Sunset

LANDSCAPING WITH STONE

BY HAZEL WHITE AND THE EDITORS OF SUNSET BOOKS

SUNSET BOOKS • MENLO PARK, CALIFORNIA

SIMPLE AND PERMANENT

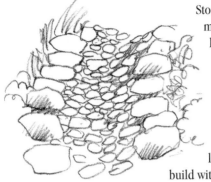

Stone, the stuff our earth is made of, is now the trendiest of building materials for the garden. Unlike most of our surroundings, it is natural, simple, and enduring, and it harmonizes beautifully, needless to say, with plants and water.

Because of the variety of stone available—hard, dark, craggy igneous rocks such as granite and basalt, sedimentary sandstones and limestones formed by the movement of water or wind and painted by nature in a multitude of pretty colors, and metamorphic slate and marble—you can build with stone to create a wide range of effects. In the process, you can't help but capture something deeply evocative of the natural landscape. The stone looks immortal, the passage of time is etched on its surface, and a tiny plant growing in a crevice is a reminder of the struggle of living things. This book shows the many ways you can use stone in your garden. It explains how to build with this unique material, how to shop for stone, and which plants complement it best.

We would like to thank Victor Thomas of Lyngso Garden Materials, Redwood City, California, for his suggestions while reviewing the manuscript; Philip Johnson, Walnut Creek, California, for his comments; and John R. Dunmire, Los Altos, California, for reviewing the sections on rock garden plants. We are especially grateful to Bill Gorgas, San Francisco stonemason, for sharing his knowledge of stone with us.

SUNSET BOOKS

Vice President and General Manager: Richard A. Smeby

Editorial Director: Bob Doyle

Production Director: Lory Day

Art Director: Vasken Guiragossian

Staff for this book:

Managing Editor: Marianne Lipanovich

Sunset Books Senior Editor, Gardening: Suzanne Normand Eyre

Copy Editor and Indexer: Margaret E. Hines

Photo Researcher: Tishana Peebles

Production Coordinator: Patricia S. Williams

Assistant Editors: Lisa Anderson, Bridget Biscotti Bradley, Barbara Brown

Art Director: Alice Rogers

Illustrator: Rik Olson

Computer Production: Joan Olson, Linda Bouchard, Deborah Cowder

Cover: Photography by Renee Lynn, Davis/Lynn Images. Garden design by Bob Clark and Raul Zumba, Oakland, California. Border photograph by Norman A. Plate. Cover production by Jean Warboy.

PHOTOGRAPHERS:

Dan Boroff: 10 bottom, 30, 31 bottom right, 65 top right; **Marion Brenner:** 121 top; **Kathleen Brenzel:** 118 center; **Jack Chandler:** 29 top left; **Peter Christiansen:** 113 bottom, 114 top; **Grey Crawford:** 75 top; **Claire Curran:** 58 top left; **Arnaud Descat/M.A.P.:** 32 bottom, 61 top left; **William B. Dewey:** 61 bottom left, 124 bottom; **Macduff Everton:** 28 top; **Derek Fell:** 66 top; **John Glover/The Garden Picture Library:** 77 bottom left; **Harold Greer:** 124 middle top; **Mick Hales/GreenWorld Pictures:** 31 top left; **Harry Haralambou:** 38, 49 bottom right; **Pamela Harper:** 20 top right, 22 bottom, 27 bottom right, 45 top right, 57 top right, bottom right, 67 top left, 68 top, bottom, 69 bottom left, 71 bottom left, 71 bottom right; **Lynne Harrison:** 24 right, 55 bottom left, 65 bottom left, 71 top right, 73 top left; **Philip Harvey:** 34 top, 85 top, 113 top, 114 bottom, 115 bottom; **Saxon Holt:** 3 top, 4–5, 7 top right, 9 bottom left, bottom right, 11 top, bottom, 13 middle right, bottom, 15 top left, top right, 19 top right, 21 bottom left, 27 top right, 35 top left, bottom left, 36 top, 41 top left, 42 top, 44 top, 48, 49 top left, 51 bottom left, 52, 53 bottom, 56 top, 59 top right, 60, 66 bottom right, 67 bottom, 72 top, 73 top right, bottom left, 75 bottom left, bottom right, 76 top, 103; **James F. Housel:** 112 top; **judywhite/New Leaf Images:** 25 top left; **Matthew Lawson:** 29 bottom; **Allan Mandell:** 1, 3 middle, 12 top, 21 bottom right, 37 bottom left, 39 top left, 40 bottom, 56 bottom, 59 bottom right, 64, 65 top left, 69 top, 72 bottom, 73 bottom right, 77 top left, 78–79, 126 middle bottom; **Charles Mann:** 19 bottom, 35 bottom right, 37 top right, 58 bottom, 70 bottom, 74 top, 123 middle top, 126 top; **Zara McCalmont/The Garden Picture Library:** 46 bottom; **Jim McCausland:** 121 bottom; **David McDonald/PhotoGarden, Inc.:** 21 top right, 45 bottom right, 49 top right, 57 bottom left, 119 middle, bottom, 120 top, 121 middle; **N. and P. Mioulane/M.A.P.:** 7 bottom left, 8 top, 43 bottom, 44 bottom, 53 top right, 63 bottom right; **Yann Monel/M.A.P.:** 10 top, 17 top left, 45 top left; **Ncum/M.A.P.:** 22 top; **Hugh Palmer:** 7 top left, 16 top, 17 top, 23 bottom, 24 left, 25 top right, 26 bottom, 32 top, 53 top left, 55 top, 71 top left, 76 bottom, 77 bottom right, back cover top left; **Jerry Pavia:** 8 bottom, 12 middle, 13 top left, 14 top, bottom, 15 bottom, 17 top right, 18 bottom, 20 top left, bottom, 21 top left, 25 bottom, 28 bottom, 29 top right, 31 top right, bottom left, 34 bottom, 35 top right, 39 top right, 40 top, 42 bottom, 43 top right, top left, 45 bottom left, 47 bottom left, bottom right, 50 top, 51 top left, top right, 54 top, 62 top, 63 top left, top right, bottom left, 65 bottom right, 69 bottom right, 77 top right, 91 top right, 126 middle top, back cover bottom left; **Norman A. Plate:** 70 top; **Matthew Plut:** 12 bottom, 19 top left, 23 top left, 33 top right, 33 bottom, 49 bottom left, 55 bottom right, 57 top left, 58 top right, 59 top left, 67 top right, 74 bottom, 83, 85 bottom, 87, 95, 105, back cover top right; **Rob Proctor:** 9 top, 36 bottom; **Bill Ross:** 3 bottom, 68 middle, 110–111, 112 bottom, 115 top; **Susan A. Roth:** 7 bottom right, 16 bottom, 23 top right, 26 top, 33 top left, 37 top left, bottom right, 39 bottom right, 41 top right, 46 top, 47 top right, 50 bottom, 62 bottom, 101, 122, 123 bottom; **Chad Slattery:** 18 top, 118 top; **Randy & Kara Stephens-Flemming:** 54 bottom; **Joseph G. Strauch, Jr.:** 126 bottom; **Michael S. Thompson:** 39 bottom left, 61 top right, 66 bottom left, 124 top, middle bottom; **Deidra Walpole Photography:** 6, 27 top left; **Darrow Watt:** 123 top; **Peter O. Whiteley:** 41 bottom, 47 top left; **Doug Wilson:** 118 bottom; **Tom Woodward:** 119 top, 123 middle bottom; **Tom Wyatt:** 91 top left, bottom.

Project Designs: Heide Stolpestad Baldwin: 85 bottom; **Dan Boroff Landscape:** 87, 95; **Delaney & Cochran:** 85 top; **Isabelle Greene & Associates:** 103; **Harland Hand:** 105; **Ron Herman:** 83.

CONTENTS

A GUIDE TO
DESIGN

Stone is natural and timeless. In its unprocessed form—gravels and boulders straight from the rivers, fields, or mountains—it brings an exceptionally natural look to the garden. And yet, when stone is either crushed for use underfoot or trimmed for paving and wall work, it can also be supremely elegant. For these reasons, stone is often the first choice in any garden design project.

In this chapter, you'll find examples of the ways designers and garden owners have used stone for building the structural elements of the garden—its paths and steps, walls and patios—and also the garden's ornamental attractions—its water features, flower gardens, and sculptural accents. There are hundreds of tips here on what makes a stone feature beautiful and how to translate these ideas into your own garden.

As you'll see, well-chosen stone has the quality of always seeming to belong. It often evokes an atmosphere of simplicity and serenity. But it can also be used playfully, or to make a sophisticated, bold, contemporary garden.

A stone path between stone walls leads into a tunnel of trumpet vine *(Clytostoma)*. Walking here in the sunshine, you'd feel the warmth of the stones change to coolness in the shade.

Design: Gary Fredericks

PATHS AND STEPS

All paths are tracks for the eyes, not just the feet. They determine how people see and experience the garden. While you are thinking about each stone path in your garden—should it go this way or that, how wide should it be, what material should it be made of, should there be an arch over it, should it slope or should there be steps—remember that you are planning a unique journey for the people who will walk along it.

In the following pages you will see many examples of how garden designers and owners have created a journey along a stone path. Generally, designers start at the house with a broad main path of a formal material and take this path to the garden's primary destination. If the house is formal and elegant, cut stone might be the paving choice. If the house is a cottage or a cabin, the path might be of rough fieldstone instead.

Once you've connected the main path to the house, using a paving material that doesn't offend the architecture, you're free to create any kind of journey through the garden you please. Break up the journey occasionally, making it seem longer and more interesting, by changing the paving material as the path moves into a different area of the garden. Create subsidiary paths off the main path; make them smaller, less formal, and less elaborate. As a rule of thumb, step down the formality the farther you get from the house; for example, switch from cut stone to flagstone, or from fieldstone to gravel as you proceed deeper into the garden. At the farthest point from the house, on a trail off a subsidiary path, you might be leading people along stepping-stones that end at a secret bench or with a view from the garden toward the hills.

While you are planning, bear in mind who is likely to walk your path. Will they enjoy the irregular, moss-covered stepping-stones or do you need a more secure surface underfoot in that part of the garden? The rougher the surface, the slower people will walk. Vary the pace through the garden according to the purpose of the path; make a smooth surface for people arriving at the front door, a more irregular surface for a slow amble through the rose garden.

If you have a sloping garden, consider it an opportunity for more variety. A change in level creates interest, which is why designers often incorporate a couple of steps into a path where they aren't strictly necessary. Many of the garden steps shown in the following pages serve primarily an aesthetic purpose: they are an excuse to introduce a second, perhaps contrasting, type of stone along the path; or to create a series of strong, crisp lines in an informal garden; or simply to decorate the path and add drama to the journey through the garden.

FACING PAGE: If you have a ready supply of affordable stone, consider using it for all your garden projects. On a rocky hillside in Santa Barbara, California, stone from the site was cut and laid as a staircase into the slope, between walls of bedrock. Buff-colored boulders, also from the site, decorate the steep meadow gardens. The entrance path, in the foreground, is French limestone, interrupted by strips of fragrant thyme.

Landscape architect: Van Atta Associates

A flagstone path follows the garden boundary, which is often a quiet, sheltered, forgotten place with pretty views back across the garden.

A straight path with an enchanting destination in sight pulls you directly into the garden. Make sure there's a little secondary interest, such as these topiary forms entwined with morning glory *(Convolvulus),* to slow down the journey.

Thick pieces of flagstone as large as these can be laid directly on the soil, providing the soil doesn't heave after frosts. Large pieces of stone also make a more gracious path than a patchwork of fragments. A white-flowered bellflower *(Campanula)* is beginning to soften the edges of the stone.

Design: Conni Cross

Squared granite setts, or cobblestones, laid in circles pave the way to the door. Over the threshold, the indoor floor picks up the same pattern.

FLAGSTONE AND FIELDSTONE PATHS

Solid stone paths of fieldstone or flagstone have a natural, understated elegance. They are easier to walk on than stepping-stones and more elaborate than gravel. For rugged paths in the more remote parts of the garden, choose fieldstone. Save flagstone for the high-traffic areas close to the house.

A path of fieldstone, perhaps collected from the site, follows the lay of the land through this shady natural garden. The stones are rough enough to provide a safe walking surface on the slope; steps would have added drama and made a less tranquil scene.

For the best-looking path, lay the largest pieces of stone on the path edges, the smaller pieces in the center.

Straight sides and an edging of society garlic *(Tulbaghia violacea)* provide some formality to a flagstone path leading to the house. Although you can't see the front door, the signs are clear that you are on the right path.

The effect of nature reclaiming a path and a wall on the edge of the garden is so romantic it's worth copying. Let the paving stones tilt and sink and the moss and wildflowers seed themselves from the banks into the irregular spaces between the stones. It's unlikely that anyone will trip as the sense of wildness and need for care is so clear.

The designer chose an Arizona sandstone (a shade called buckskin) for a path that wraps around the house against a sloping garden decorated with native boulders. Set on a concrete slab with mortared joints, the path is flat enough for furniture where it opens up into a patio. Contractors sawed the stone to fit as they laid it.

Design: Heide Stolpestad Baldwin

Although the fieldstone path crosses the threshold into the vegetable garden without any change in the paving to alert you that you are entering a different space, the fragrant angel's trumpet *(Brugmansia)* arching over the gateway provides a reason to pause here in the dappled shade for a moment and catch a pretty view of the garden ahead.

Design: Gary Fredericks

Flagstone and Fieldstone Paths 9

Dip the center of a rough path to suggest age and wear, or to make the path look as if it's following the contours of a naturally occurring low spot.

The best designs often originate from having to make do. If there's only local stone and it's irregular in size and shape, the gardener might use it as shown here. The very largest, flattest stone makes a landing under the arch. Other large stone pieces are trimmed to make an elegant path near the house. The rough stone is reserved for a path on the outskirts of the garden; the pieces form a patchwork, with violas and lady's-mantle *(Alchemilla mollis)* growing in the seams.

The designer chose geometric cut stone for a patio close to the house and irregular flagstone for the path that leads away from the patio and through the garden to the back gate. The transition between the two stone shapes—both bluestone—was effected by cutting the flagstones that butted the patio so that they had straight edges on the patio side.

Design: Dan Borroff Landscape

The entrance to this shortcut from the driveway to the house is marked by the boulder and the column of juniper in the foreground. Made of local stone, the same as the boulder, the path flows through the garden, turning past repeated clumps of bearded iris and blue fescue *(Festuca ovina* 'Glauca'). A light-colored gravel is packed between the stones.

A straight path of fieldstone, edged with the same stone, seems perfectly natural in a vegetable garden where the corn, beans, and dahlias are in straight lines, too. As you're deciding whether a path should be straight or curved, take your cue from the lines in the surrounding landscape.

Design: Gary Fredericks

STEPPING-STONE PATHS

A stepping-stone path encourages a slow, reflective walk. Place one in a part of the garden where nobody would want to rush, and create reasons—a close view of water, an unusual flower, a sweet fragrance—for pausing at every step.

Great stepping-stone paths have rhythm. Instead of placing stones one behind the other in a straight line, arrange them in groups, and within each group set the stones zigzagging loosely off the center line. A stone with a convex surface, like the stone in the foreground here, seems to taper off into bedrock. Because the stones are raised above the moss, there's a lovely sense of crossing over it.

To make the stones flow, lay a straight edge of one stone against a straight edge of another, a concave edge against a convex edge.

In fall and winter, a simple, raised stepping-stone path suggests a walk beneath the bare trees. If the stones weren't here, there would be no easy way to cross the seasonal mud, and no invitation to come out and smell the last leaves after a rain.

At the entrance to a stepping-stone path and at any stopping place along the way, consider broadening the path into a mini-terrace of stones so there's space for people to gather and stay awhile. The pool of stones here marks the start of the path outside the front door. The first step in the staircase up through the yarrow lawn is an inviting extralarge stone.

Design: Heide Stolpestad Baldwin

As you're planning a path, work in the prepositions—the more, the better. For example, to be natural looking, a winding path must turn around something. Here the path goes around boulders, by a slope splashed with gold rudbeckias and red sedum, between low mounds of juniper and then tall clumps of miscanthus grass, and out through and under the canopies of trees.

In this Japanese-style garden, composed almost entirely of stone, a blue-gray gravel stream winds its way through a narrow space between the house and the garden wall. The banks of the stream are made of coarser tan gravel; boulders sit on the stream edge, making a gorge for the water to flow through. Stepping-stones—large, thick, irregular slabs of rock—run through the garden, carrying you across the water.

Landscape architect: Isabelle Greene & Associates

Stepping-stones set in ground cover make an uneven surface that needs to be well lit if it will be used in the evening. On sunny days, the journey along this path is beautiful because of the natural light: you travel through a cool tunnel of dappled moving shade under the trees and then out into the bright, open meadow of snow-in-summer *(Cerastium tomentosum)* by the gate.

A stepping-stone path planted with woolly thyme *(Thymus pseudolanuginosus)* and edged with Santa Barbara daisy *(Erigeron karvinskianus)* sets an intimate, cottagey scale through part of this garden. It then opens up into a patio, where people can stop and admire the garden together. Note the repetition of soft mounding forms in the garden.

Design: Sarah Hammond

Have the path meander over, between, under, alongside, and around other garden elements to slow the journey through the garden.

A low, tight ground cover between stepping-stones highlights the shape of each stone, especially if the ground cover is bright or dark green. The shapes of individual stones are less noticeable if the plant foliage is close in color to the stone color and are lost among loose plants that billow over their edges.

Stepping-stones can save a lawn or sensitive ground cover from too much wear at a high-traffic point, and they can provide access to the garden in wet weather. Arrange the stones to emphasize the swing through a pergola *(left)* or to steer people across the lawn *(above left)*. Lay them in a distinctive pattern *(above right)* to particularly catch the eye.

GRAVEL PATHS

Clean gravels crunch or click underfoot. Gravels that include the fine particles and dust from the crushing process make a sandy and almost silent surface. Either type can be designed to look formal, with an arch or symmetrical edgings of boxwood or lavender, or to look like bedrock, with the edgings lost among wildflowers.

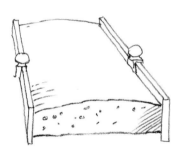

Make a crown with an extra inch of gravel in the path center to give the surface a little more interest.

The gravel path and box *(Buxus)* hedges are covered with the yellow petals of a goldenchain tree *(Laburnum)* in late spring and fallen leaves in autumn. This path is designed for a gardener who loves raking — and the enchanting feeling of walking in the shelter of trees.

A path that curves away out of view has mystery — an important element in garden design, because it draws people through the garden. Note the grace of the curve in this brown gravel path; there is nothing wriggly about it. The golden-leafed shrub on the outside of the curve draws the eye and the feet automatically follow through the first section of the path to the curve. At that point, as you turn, another eye-catching plant, a bench, or a piece of sculpture probably comes into view. The path is edged with benderboard.

Design: Tom Pellet

Providing a resting place along a path extends people's perception of the journey. This is a useful trick in a small garden with room for only a short path. From the bench, people's eyes are drawn away from the path and across the garden to enjoy a new view, again enlarging the sense of the garden.

To accommodate a four-foot bench graciously, make the setback off the path six feet long and three feet deep. Flank the bench with colorful flowers, such as these sunflowers *(Helianthus)* and California poppies *(Eschscholzia californica),* or with a fragrant shrub or a simple water bowl. Don't forget to place something across from the bench in the garden as a focal point for the view.

An upright boulder marks the entrance to a path through a grove of maples. Even in the most natural areas of a garden, a marker of some kind is in order. It promises that there's some purpose to this path, that if you follow it you won't be disappointed. In a more formal setting, the entrance to a path might be marked with a carved stone piece, a water urn, or flowerpots.

Gravel is the conventional paving material for parterres and knot gardens. It's easy to lay in curves, and it makes a quiet foil to the fancy patterns and elaborate shapes of the topiaries.

Encroached upon by wildflowers, winding under trees and around a boulder, this decomposed granite path resembles a hiking trail in wild chaparral country. It's a beautiful illusion created by Scott Goldstein and Lauren Gabor in their garden in the heart of urban Los Angeles.

Place a solid stone apron at the doorstep so that gravel doesn't travel on people's shoes into the house, where it might scratch floors.

An unpretentious path of gray gravel runs along a border of old-fashioned flowers such as Shasta daisy *(Chrysanthemum maximum),* alyssum, roses, and ranunculus. The pebble edge to the path is mostly decorative; the gravel has spilled into the flower beds and seeds from the flowers have scattered onto the path and started to germinate there, making an enchanting topsy-turvy, cottage-garden effect.

A buff-colored decomposed granite path matches the color of the boulders holding back the hillside. The plants were also chosen to complement the rock work. The barberry *(Berberis)* in the foreground, for example, is the same blood red as the striations in the tan stone.

Design: Keeyla Meadows

A slab of flagstone set in a decomposed granite path marks the threshold at the gateway to this garden. Threshold stones are common in old European gardens. They are often larger than this and serve the same kind of purpose as elbow patches: they prevent the path from becoming threadbare at the point where it's most used.

Design: Chris Jacobson

Narrow and worn-looking, like a sheep track, this path runs quietly through the garden. Note the dip in the path and the way the path runs alongside the fence, then at the last minute jags over and through the gate, hiding the new view until then.

Design: Daniel Forest

PATHS OF MIXED MATERIALS

Paths of mixed materials catch the eye. They invite people to delight in the shape of a naturally river-washed stone lying among broken fieldstones or in the many different hues of varicolored sharp gravel between smooth blue pebbles. The contrasts in materials can be bold or subtle, according to your style.

Paving composed of repeated geometric units comes to life if you add natural rounded stone. The blue, gray, and tan pebbles between these concrete pavers *(above)* are color coordinated with the varicolored gravel seeded into the concrete's surface. Dark pebbles *(right)* make a bold contrasting pattern between old cobblestones.

The two-tone brick panel is as directional as an arrow. It points the way through a narrow space into the sun-filled garden beyond. It also provides a flat, easy surface for walking; small round pebbles are uncomfortable to walk on, so they are best used for decoration, as they have been here.

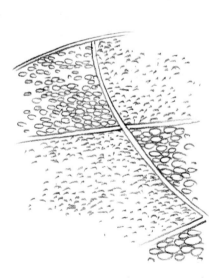

Decorate a concrete surface, as you pour it, with an elegant pattern of two different types and sizes of pebbles.

A path of flat pebbles and fieldstones moves like a stream, curving around a high bank and running quietly under overhanging foliage. Consider using the soil you excavate to make the path foundation for banks on one or both sides of the path. It's more interesting to walk between banks than through an entirely flat area, plants are better displayed on a bank, and a small berm on the edges makes the path invisible from another part of the garden.

A garden can be used to display stone as well as plants. Pebbles, cobbles, fieldstones, and slabs of different types of flagstone are patched together in this path. Roughly cut fieldstones edge the sides, and in among the plants lie washes of pebbles, occasional boulders, and a scree of large, red ochre rocks.

Japanese paths often combine subtly different materials. Two shades of stone, a combination of new and old stone, a stone with a straight-cut edge alongside a stone split or naturally broken—details like these make a path delightful without overwhelming a quiet composition of green foliage.

A path from the street to the front door offers pedestrians a stroll through the front garden instead of entering by the driveway. The design plays with soft gray textures: fine, sharp gravel pieces lie between alternating bands of roughly squared old cobblestones and smooth water-washed flagstone.

Design: Suzanne Porter

Cut Stone Paths

Cut stone can be straitlaced formal or playful in its geometry. Either way, it makes a flat, regular walking surface particularly suitable for entrances and main walkways.

Change cut stone to gravel or fieldstone at the entrance to a less formal part of the garden. Place a threshold stone where they meet.

A change in paving material is a cue. Stepping off the main cut stone walkway with its geometric formality and broad dimensions onto a smaller gravel path, you know for sure that you're leaving the house and the main traffic routes behind and entering the quiet world of the garden.

The band of cut stone crossing the gravel walk halfway down its length promises an intersection. You'll have an opportunity there to leave this intimate, sheltered walk for a formal walkway that will march you back toward a more public part of the garden.

The strong solid shapes of the cut stone paving provide a counterpoint to the billowing plants and drifting petals. The sense of order the straight lines bring accentuates the naturalness of the flowers.

Closely laid, cut bluestone makes an elegant, practical walking surface. No one is likely to trip on the way to the house, even in twilight or carrying groceries. And cut stone, unlike deep gravel, is kind to guests' soft leather shoes and to wheelchairs and wheelbarrows. In keeping with the style of the house, the path was laid a little informally, with its edges following the flowing lines of the plantings.

Design: Judy Ogden

A generous scale makes a garden feel gracious. This cut stone path is 8½ feet wide, which allows two people to amble side by side between the rows of clipped myrtles *(Myrtus communis)* in pots. This is not a large garden; the path ends here by a pool that touches the garden fence.

Design: Marta Fry Landscape Architects

The hopscotch pattern of cut stone in the gravel draws the eye to the bench in the distance and provides textural interest to the path, particularly useful during the many months when the roses aren't in bloom. Each time you move off the stone to smell a rose, your step registers pleasantly in the sound of the gravel crunching underfoot. Notice that the joints between the pairs of stone on the path are staggered; too much symmetry would be out of place in this informal part of the garden.

Arrange cut stones so the lines of the joints make L's and T's. Avoid crosses, which break up the flow of the design.

Low-growing plants between cut stone rectangles soften the edges of the stone and emphasize the pattern. Note the brick edging, which ties in the path with the brick house.

Design: Katzman/Lilly Design

Like the hopscotch walk on the previous page, this path is composed of two materials that sound, and also feel, very different underfoot. Unless the grass is frosty, the sound of footsteps stops as someone moves from stone to soft grass. Practically, the pattern pulls your eye across a wide, distracting driveway to what the garden designer wants you to see: a bench among roses, set back between flanking trees. Consider, too, that if the expense of a broad cut stone path is a concern, a panel of grass offers substantial savings.

Where there are both formal and informal, architectural and natural elements in the landscape, cut stone combined with fieldstone or gravel links the two together. Large slabs of cut stone also make elegant steps.

Being roughly cut, cobble-stones (*above* and *left*) make more informal-looking paths than sawn cut stone and are thus more useful for small paths that lead away from the main traffic routes in the garden. Like brick, cobble-stones can be laid in various patterns.

STEPS AND STAIRCASES

Steps are a strong design element in a garden. Well-designed steps are extremely inviting. They make a series of bold, horizontal lines up the garden, calling attention to the change in topography. It is best to underplay them using simple stone with little if any adornment. If the grade is steep, create landings between short flights of stairs, and give people plenty of excuses to pause and take in the view.

These are stepping-stone stairs on a grand leisurely scale—a step and then a landing, another step, another landing. The slope is gentle enough that the steps might not have been necessary from a purely practical standpoint, but the architectural lines of the risers swing beautifully up the slope, inviting you into the garden.

Design: Conni Cross

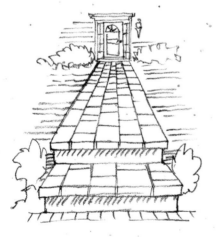

Create an invitation on an entrance path with two small steps. Make the treads at least 15 inches deep for comfort, and at least 5 feet wide to allow two people to walk side by side.

Stone and brick, the two hardscape materials in this garden, are married in the steps. Although the steps are steep, the garden at the top of them promises to be worth the climb.

A single step, composed of two or three slabs of rock, breaks the downhill flow of a steep gravel path. The same type of rock appears as boulders in the garden and as an edging to the path. Note the complementary colors of step and path and the beautiful contrast in texture—the two feel quite different underfoot.

These steps in a rocky hillside garden could almost have been carved out of bedrock. The sharp edges are hidden in mats of thyme *(Thymus),* and the steps seem to go this way and that to avoid a spill of boulders. Note the pleasing lines made by the various widths of the risers.

Landscape architect: Van Atta Associates

Weaving steps across a slope, even just a little, takes some of the effort out of a climb. Only a few steps are ever in view, so the climb is taken in stages, with stops at every corner as a different part of the path and garden come into view. In this herb garden, the fragrances released by the plants bordering the path also distract attention away from the climb.

A broad entry walk consists of an unusual combination of Italian tile and pea gravel. The tile steps bring the color and horizontal lines of the architecture out into the landscape, settling the house into the land. The stretches of pea gravel diminish the formality. Note the gracious dimensions of the steps: tiny risers, deep treads. The steps could have been at least twice as high, but then there would have been fewer steps, and consequently, fewer reasons to pause. The extra steps draw out the experience of arriving at the house through a madrone forest full of moss-covered boulders.

Landscape architect:
Jack Chandler & Associates

A tall stone wall alongside a path provides a pleasant sense of shelter. It's also an opportunity to display rock plants and stone at eye level. The treads of the steps are tied to the downhill slope in a mat of creeping and woolly thyme *(Thymus)*.

For drama, run steps straight up and down the slope. For an easier climb and to draw out the journey, zigzag the steps across the slope.

Boulders culled from the ground during construction break up the edges of this concrete entrance staircase. First, the steps were roughly excavated. Next, twine and stakes were set out to mark the exact shape of the finished steps. The boulders were then positioned, the twine serving as a guide to where the concrete would be. The concrete forms were built around the boulders, and the concrete was poured into the forms, right up to the rock.

Landscape architect:
Jack Chandler & Associates

A concrete path can be transformed with stone detailing. The risers of the steps in this path are laid like stacked stone walls; the same stone is inlaid on the circular landing, where the path from the driveway joins the main path, and also on the veranda at the front door.

A stepping-stone staircase is one of the simplest ways to take a path up a slope. The stairs are built from the bottom up, the back of each stone supporting the tip of the stone above it. Note the thickness of the stones and the generous size of the treads. Once the stones are bedded well into the hillside, their weight will help keep them stable.

PATIOS AND SITTING PLACES

When planning a stone-paved patio or sitting area, bear in mind that any successful outdoor living space, whether it's for dining or lounging, has two essential features: It is open to the sky and the sun so that you feel close to nature—sunlight plays across the furniture and sparkles on the glasses, a breeze riffles through the leaves, and there's a fragrance of flowers or ripe fruit in the air. And it is roomlike—at least in some way—so that you can comfortably live in it as you do indoors: eating, sleeping, talking, or enjoying an hour of solitude.

Carefully look at each possible location for an outdoor dining or sitting space. Is there privacy or could privacy be arranged with a screen of plants or a trellis? Is there a view? What sounds do you hear? How is the light at different times of the day? Is there a welcome breeze or too much of a breeze? The natural feel of the place is the most important consideration, so even if it is most convenient to place the outdoor dining area off the kitchen, assess the characteristics of that location before you build.

The outdoor living areas pictured on the following pages show many ways to make a space roomlike. Some take advantage of a house wall or a boundary fence to help enclose the space, or they use hedges or a collection of plants in pots to define the area. The spaces are defined further by a durable, all-weather stone floor suitable for furniture. In hot climates there's often something of a ceiling: a lightly branched tree canopy, an awning or umbrella, or a lightly planted arbor. A deciduous tree is particularly useful, because it will shade the area in summer and let sunlight through in winter.

Create several living areas in the garden, perhaps one large area for entertaining and smaller sitting places positioned to take advantage of the shade of a tree, a view, a chance of solitude, or a pool of sunshine against a warm wall. Or wrap a patio around two sides of the house, so that you may have some shade on one side while the other side is in the sun.

If the patio is close to the house, relate the size of the patio to the size of the inside rooms, but go somewhat larger in deference to the grander scale of the outdoors. Use materials that link the patio to the indoors; for example, lay cut stone in both the kitchen and the outdoor dining room, or put metal furniture in both, or continue the colors of the indoor room outside using flowers or table linens. In hot summer climates, avoid white furniture and very pale stone floors because of the glare.

Choose comfortable furniture and plan how you will store it if need be. For a refuge in the heart of your garden, closest to nature, you might forget about shopping in traditional outlets and instead make the furniture with stone slabs and boulders.

FACING PAGE: It's just a few steps from someone's office to this formal sitting area overlooking Lake Steilacoom, Washington. The pavers are made of cast stone (concrete) textured and acid-stained to look like real stone. The gravel beds are crushed basalt.

Design: Dan Borroff Landscape

Romantically hidden in the woods, this picnic place might be the destination of a path at the farthest point from the house. The walls shelter it from the wind, and it has a solid stone floor, but the roof lets in every cheery beam of woodland light.

Water-eroded rocks edge this Chinese cobblestone terrace. The paving is traditionally made by placing tiles on edge in a bed of sand to create the partitions within the pattern and filling the patterns tightly with pebbles, splinters of stone, colored glass, and fragments of white teacups. A mix of sand and dry cement swept into the paving and lightly watered helps set the materials in place.

A gravel entrance courtyard doubles as a dining area. There's room for six comfortable chairs around the table, and behind the chairs, room for people to take their places at the table graciously, without backing into the flower beds.

Design: Sarah Hammond

Situated on the sheltered south side of the house, this patio of "Montana slate" was added with the simple objective of making a space for the owners to be in the garden, to sit outside on a fine day. A small patio on the windy east side was rarely used.

Design: Dan Borroff Landscape

OUTDOOR DINING AREAS

An outdoor dining room needs a sturdy even floor or the furniture will wobble, and there should be ample space for people to move about and seat themselves. A site close to the kitchen is convenient for entertaining; a site away from the house may take advantage of a view or a breeze. In a small garden, try fashioning a dining space at a path intersection or an entrance area.

Two-tone stone paving and color-coordinated furniture decorate this sheltered patio in a quiet, green garden. Note how the white mortar between the stones highlights the stone shapes; if the mortar had been stained to match the color of the stone, the overall shape of the patio would have caught the eye instead.

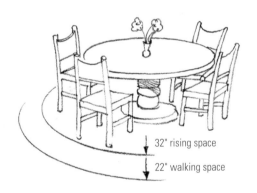

32" rising space

22" walking space

Allow at least 4½ feet of clearance all around the dining table. The more room there is, the more gracious the space will feel.

The most common place for a dining patio is adjacent to the house. The house wall shelters the patio on one side, and the patio is convenient to the kitchen. Here, tightly laid concrete pavers seeded with varicolored small pebbles make a simple-to-lay, economical floor. Moss has infiltrated the cracks between the pavers and spread into the pebbles.

Four colors flicker in a random pattern like dappled light across a large patio of simple, rectangular cut stone. The dining tables have been set up close to the view and in a position likely to catch a summer breeze. For a more intimate setting, a table might be moved into the foreground, where the patio is sheltered by the high wall.

Design: Conni Cross

This outdoor dining room is bounded by four "walls": two house walls (the patio sits in an L), a bank in the foreground, and a grand, columned walkway that leads away from the house to the pool and on toward the boundary of the garden. Part of the patio is shaded by the cascading Lady Banks' rose *(Rosa banksiae)* growing on the columns of the walkway and trained across the patio on overhead wires. The mortared flagstone is edged with Mexican tile. The same materials are used in the walkway, but there the gaps between the flagstones are planted with fragrant violets *(Viola)*.

Design: gardenmakers

In a small garden, a patio might be no more than a generous space where two or more paths meet. A dining table and chairs can be kept tucked along one side and moved out across the path when lunch is ready. Note how the blue in the furniture matches the blue tiles in the paving, the blue flowers, and the design in the pot, successfully tying those different elements together in a small space.

Design: Keeyla Meadows

SITTING PLACES

An ideal outdoor sitting space is comfortable and sheltered. It is sited very particularly to catch a view or the sunshine late in the day. On a grand terrace the length of the house, there's room for a couch and some armchairs, perhaps a lounger in the shade of an oak, and a stool against a warm wall for morning coffee. In smaller gardens, make a retaining wall, boulder, or log double as an occasional seat.

Granite blocks double as sculptural accents and occasional seating on this partially grouted, partially planted Arizona flagstone patio. On the side of the patio facing the natural landscape is a fence made of peeler logs and manzanita branches.

Landscape architect: Delaney & Cochran

Choose a partially defined space for a sitting area and arrange the seats in a loose circle. People prefer to sit at an angle to one another rather than side by side.

Every room, including an outdoor room, needs a focal point. On this circular flagstone patio bounded by shrubs, the eye is drawn to the miniaturized rock garden in a raised circle capped with the same flagstone.

A stopping place among the trees, where green light dances over moss and stones and tree trunks, is magical. Find a clearing where the light penetrates the tree canopy, or make one if need be. Define the space with a threshold stone and a circle of boulders to serve as seats *(right)*, or make low walls of woodland shrubs and lay a stone floor *(above)*.

The quietest, most private place in the garden — the place that will give you the greatest sense of solitude — is one of the best spots for a bench. In hot climates, provide some shade from an overhead trellis or the canopy of a tree.

A reflection pool makes a dramatic edge to a patio. From your seat, you can watch a sparkling, upside-down view of the garden and sky that changes with the light and the season. Note the informal edging at the far side of the pool, where it meets the natural planting.

The secrets to successful crazy paving are to avoid small pieces of flagstone and to make sure the jagged edges of the stones are completely hidden. In this sitting area, creeping and woolly thyme *(Thymus praecox arcticus, Thymus pseudolanuginosus)* make a reliable, soft, fragrant mat over the stones.

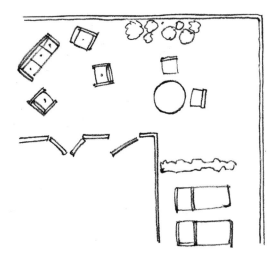

Wrap the patio around the house, separating it into different areas that correspond to the adjoining indoor rooms.

A bench and a stone mosaic spread like a circle of intricate carpet on the ground define this space sufficiently as an outdoor room and provide all the necessary ornamentation. The mosaic darkens and shines after rain; in some places, patches of moss have spread into the pattern.

Garden furniture should be comfortable above all else. Try it at the store before you place an order. Consider also how much maintenance the furniture may need and whether you'll need to store it in winter. Teak and redwood are both strong, rot-resistant woods (for environmental preservation reasons, purchase only plantation-grown teak and recycled redwood) and turn a soft gray as they weather.

The light is soft and dappled here on the bench under the trees, and the boulders at each side provide a pleasant sense of enclosure. Like all great sitting places, the bench is protected yet commands a view. Angle your sitting area so that your gaze is directed toward the best part of the garden.

Place seats where you want people to stop and admire the garden. Set them so that the backs are against something if you can, even if it's as low as the rock garden here. In cool climates, place them to face the sun.

Design: Conni Cross

A patio of geometric concrete pavers is formal where it joins the house, but here at the other side it fuses with a natural-looking landscape dominated by boulders. Note how the boulders are anchored by grasses placed in front of them.

Design: The Berger Partnership

WALLS

The practical reasons for building a stone wall are to retain a bank of soil or to make a secure, solid, long-lasting barrier that screens out wind and noise. But it's the other reasons—the aesthetic and psychological ones—that explain why designers can find a use for a stone wall in almost any garden.

A stone wall brings an unmatched sense of permanence to the garden, and in contrast to that timeless quality, the plants growing against it or in it appear softer, their flowers more ephemeral. A stone wall adjoining the house extends the lines of the architecture out into the garden and settles the house into the land. A wall can create a positive outdoor space by defining the boundary and by making a backdrop for the furniture and plantings. Most important perhaps is the sense of shelter and comfort a wall provides; a wall embraces a space and separates it from the outside world. The word "paradise" derives from a Persian word meaning "a walled place."

The photographs on the following pages show some of the variety of stone walls. Most romantic is a crumbling stone wall that is becoming overgrown with roses. Most formal is a veneered cut stone wall at the entrance to a driveway. Most playful is a series of massive cut boulders and stone slabs piled into a line along the edge of a lawn. Prettiest are the dry-laid walls planted with rock garden plants.

Be sure to study the effect of the stone's size and shape, its color, and the pattern in which it is laid. Even low stone walls can appear monumental if the stone is uniformly large, dark, and regularly coursed (laid with long horizontal joint lines). Small stones help to make a tall wall look less massive. Loose, billowing plants and the flickering shadows from nearby trees will soften a wall that is a little oppressive looking. If you need a tall screen in a small space, consider building a low stone wall and topping it with a fence. This will give you the privacy you need without overwhelming the space.

The best walls in small gardens are usually low ones. A wall not much higher than a curb will effectively separate different areas of the garden and make the garden seem larger. Where privacy is needed, a wall that's just waist high, with one or two strategically placed tall shrubs or grasses, will perhaps be sufficient to keep people's eyes away; and it will still be low enough to allow you to look out from your small, secluded paradise to the larger landscape beyond.

FACING PAGE: A few steps dramatized with stone walls and urns signals there's probably something interesting ahead up the slope or why else would someone have gone to so much trouble. The steps have been transformed into a gateway. You couldn't help but explore.

Potato vine *(Solanum jasminoides)* breaks up the pattern of this mortared ashlar wall. The clusters of stepping-stones are of the same stone.

Design: Pamela Burton

A window in a tall wall gives a secret-feeling view into the garden beyond. Like smaller openings, or even just the occasional missing stone, it makes the wall look less dense.

Moss pink *(Phlox subulata)* softens the top of this brownstone wall as it steps down the slope. Speedwell *(Veronica)* and English daisies *(Bellis perennis)* soften the wall base. Blocky pieces of stone like these are easier to work with than round stones.

Design: Conni Cross

A retaining wall may provide a vantage point. Be sure to place at least a bench near the edge if there's a view or a shady place under an old oak.

FREESTANDING WALLS

Walls mark boundaries, for example, where a private garden meets the wild landscape or the street, or where the formal part of the garden meets the vegetable plot. Walls also provide shelter for plants and people seeking a warm place to sit.

An opening in a wall is beautiful to walk through, and it frames a view of the garden beyond. The effect is most dramatic if the path approaches the wall at an oblique angle and the view appears just as you reach the wall. From the sizes of the stones here, you can see that creating an arch is a major undertaking.

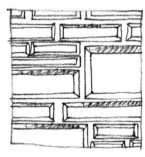

Lay ashlar stone with long horizontal joint lines for a formal effect. Break up the horizontal lines to make the ashlar look less formal.

Low walls decorated with pots of agave mark the entrance to an orange grove and the destination of the path. Without the walls, there wouldn't be the same sense of arrival or the sense of the orchard as a separate, special place.

At the edge of a stone patio high above the ground, a series of cut stone slabs installed on edge make an ingenious railing. Note the sculpted corners of the slabs.

A pillar and wall faced with cut stone at the entrance to the driveway promises an elegant property beyond. The colors of the stone and the plantings have been carefully coordinated to make a warm and vibrant welcome.

Design: Ireland-Gannon Associates

Slabs of stone arranged sculpturally on the edge of a space make a barrier that's more playful than a solid wall. The marks left by the stonemason's tools during the cutting process are evident on the faces of some of the pieces. Other pieces have naturally broken surfaces. The wall invites exploration: you can sit on it, lean against it, climb on or over it, and stand on it for a better view.

Design: Topher Delaney

A garden surrounded by a tall wall is secure and hidden from the outside world and it's protected from the sound of traffic—a tall wall keeps out traffic sound better than any other divider. If it's built of large stones, it appears monumental, perhaps even oppressive, in a small space; smaller stones and an airy climbing plant such as this 'Paul's Scarlet Climber' rose make the wall less imposing.

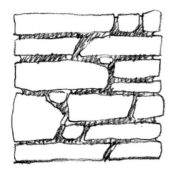

Rake the joints of a mortared wall deeply so that the mortar lies half hidden in shadow and you see more of the rock.

Walls about waist high set boundaries, but they are low enough to see over. At the same time as they establish privacy and separateness, they leave each area somewhat open to the other. In a small garden particularly, it's delightful to look out from a sheltered, walled space to a larger space beyond.

Stone pillars tied in to a low stone wall and stone steps make a dramatic entrance to this garden. The mortar between the stones is deeply raked so that it hardly shows.

A low stone wall with a bamboo or wooden fence on top of it provides a much lighter- and softer-looking screen than a solid wall of the same height, and it is less expensive to build. A bamboo fence on a stone wall is often seen in Japanese gardens. The bamboo canes are sometimes split or bamboo branches are used. The wood posts are mortared into the wall.

Even if most of the plantings are new, an old wall suggests that the garden has always been there. As long as it's safe to do so, let the wall crumble and leave the pieces where they fall. Or consider building a ruin from scratch with recycled materials.

Design: Pamela Burton

RETAINING WALLS

A stone retaining wall doesn't need to look merely functional. So much more can be made of a retaining wall that designers often create one unnecessarily on a very gentle slope. Where there's no slope at all, a raised bed provides an excuse for a stone retaining wall.

A raised bed constructed with granite walls runs along the boundary between the formal lawn and a steep woodland garden below, separating them so that they are experienced as two very different spaces. The path, hidden below the raised bed, becomes a secret path into the woods.

Plant a tree near a high retaining wall, so that the shadows of its branches will soften and break up the massive face of the wall.

A wall offers prime display space at eye level. You can use it to exhibit a plant with a strong form or texture or attach a sculpture to it — or do both, as shown here.

There's not enough of a slope in this garden to require a wall, but this wall serves an important purpose: it creates two garden areas out of one, which gives an illusion of more space—an especially useful trick in a small garden.

Architectural in its lines, natural in its plantings, this low wall helps link the house to its rural surroundings and makes a pretty boundary along the driveway. Four popular rock garden plants—basket-of-gold *(Aurinia saxatilis),* wall rockcress *(Arabis caucasica),* common aubrieta *(Aubrieta deltoidea),* and pink *(Dianthus)*—are growing well on the wall.

There are two ways to take a wall down a slope: step it down (see page 39) or build it so that the top slopes with the fall of the land.

A mortared retaining wall adjoining steps is softened by plants growing in the large gaps left at the back of each step.

A raised bed with stone walls adds interest to a flat garden, and the contents of the bed, being closer to eye level, receive more attention. As this Camperdown elm *(Ulmus glabra* 'Camperdownii') grows and its branches weep closer to the ground, the top of the wall might make a seat inside the shady tent of leaves.

Design: Philhower Nursery

An existing retaining wall that's unattractive can be masked in ivy or any other trailing or climbing, vigorous, evergreen plant. Then it becomes a quiet, green backdrop for the garden in front of it. Here, pots of topiary stand on the patio against the ivy, which doubles as an elegant collar to the stone steps.

Cap a low retaining wall to make a seat and invite people to sit among the flowers.

A low, stone retaining wall adds a little architecture to the garden and makes a striking contrast with ephemeral flowers such as these miniature daffodils and *Mazus reptans.* When the flowers are gone, the faces of the brownstone provide the decoration.

Design: Conni Cross

Being able to trim and fit stones together tightly and artfully requires professional skills. The work is hard and slow, and therefore expensive, but these walls, like old oak trees, bring a venerable quality to the garden.

Design: George Gonzales

Morning glory *(Convolvulus)* and geraniums *(Pelargonium)* cascade from the flower garden over the rubble stone wall. Mexican daisy *(Erigeron karvinskianus),* a rampant reseeder, has gained hold in some of the wall crevices.

A mortared wall offers no opportunity for plants to grow in it, but planting upright plants, such as these *Senecio mandraliscae,* at the base and billowing plants, such as California poppies *(Eschscholzia californica),* on top break up the wall face just as effectively.

WATER FEATURES

Water makes a pleasing, natural complement to stone. It is transparent and reflective, and when it moves, it sounds either soothing or exhilarating. Stone is the opposite: solid, durable, and still. Together, these contrasting elements compose some of the most beautiful scenes in nature, from a majestic waterfall in the mountains to a marsh emptying over a sandbar into the sea. Combining water and stone in the garden, even on a small scale, evokes this magical association.

In the following pages are examples of that effect. Swimming pools are edged with stone boulders like pools in the wild. Ponds and streams have pebble banks or gravelly bottoms and islands or promontories of rock. There are natural-looking waterfalls and fountains that throw the sound of chuckling, splashing, and murmuring water across the garden, and dry creekbeds that are so natural looking they seem almost to murmur. Simplest of all are the stone water bowls, which capture reflections of the sky.

People are drawn toward water. If you can site your water feature so that the water is visible from the house or can be heard from there, you may be certain of luring people outdoors into the garden. So as not to disappoint anyone, make sure that there's access right to the water's edge. For example, raise a stone water bowl to a height where the water can be touched; place a bench at the side of the pond; lead a path to a beach on the edge of the stream and place a boulder there for sitting. Only up close can someone enjoy the water's coolness, the patterns of light on the water surface, and the way the water ripples over the stone.

As you plan a water feature, consider how much light will fall on the water (the more light, the more sparkle), whether the chilling of the air will be pleasant in the garden, if the wind will carry away the fountain spray, and whether the pond will reflect the maple tree (test it out by laying a mirror on the ground and checking the reflections from different parts of the house and garden, because they'll change depending on the viewing point and the position of the sun).

For the most natural water feature, build in plenty of irregularity. Vary the edging around a pool or pond and the banks of a stream, so that there's sun and shade, shelter behind rocks or under trees, and open places that invite you to trail your hands through the water. Choose river gravels and stones with water-worn, smooth shapes to complement still or gently moving water, and stones with dynamic, sharp outlines for mountain streams and waterfalls. Look out for stones with old watermarks, colors that gleam when wet, or dimples and crevices where a moisture-loving plant might naturally seed or a miniature water reservoir collect after a rain shower.

FACING PAGE: The stepping-stone path leaves land for a brief, exciting crossing over reflections of the sky. Note the placement of pebbles and boulders to anchor the end of the bridge and the presence of other stones in the pond.

A contemporary interpretation of an old Moorish water rill, this bright streak of blue bordered by Kashmir stone and billowing rushes *(Juncus* 'Carman's Japanese') is made of glass lit from below instead of turquoise blue tile.

Design: David LeRoy Designs, Old World Builders, Tony Pastore

The flagstone edge to the koi pond and water rill bleeds into a patio area, and the same flagstone is used to cap a low stone wall seat. These touches help integrate the pond into its surroundings.

Design: Chris Jacobson

The sweet sounds of water bubbling among the rocks and rippling over the edge of the bowl carry across an urban garden. A small pump with a rigid extension pipe sits in a PVC-lined reservoir beneath the bowl.

Design: Suzanne Porter

In Japanese gardens, the main features are often stone. Here, a stepping-stone path descends the slope and becomes the edge of the stream. Stone creates the banks, the gorge, the waterfall, and even sections of the bottom of the stream. The decorative elements—bench, lantern, and frog—are also stone.

Water Features 49

Ponds and Pools

Stone islands, stone bridges, edgings of pebbles or boulders, and stone furniture and diving platforms on the water's edge—there are many opportunities for using stone in a pool or pond project.

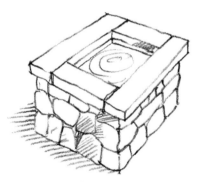

Make a raised pond by building stone walls and securing the pond liner below the stone coping.

The large boulders and the glossy abelia *(Abelia grandiflora)* tunnel the view toward a tall rock on the slope and a streambed that might be the source of the water here. The natural effect is achieved with lots of rock and a background of trees. Also, the small pond ahead of the main pond is a feature seen often in nature. Note how the streambed conveniently turns out of sight under the trees.

A sunny terrace of river rock runs right to the edge of the pool on one side. On the other side, trees and shrubs cast shadows across the water, and the pool edge becomes inaccessible at points, lost among plants and stone slabs. The kidney shape of the pool is consequently harder to trace.

Design: Conni Cross

LEFT AND BELOW RIGHT: Varying the pond edge with a stone path or a series of boulders on one side and a dense stand of reeds or a beach on another side disguises the pond's shape and makes the water more natural looking. Be sure there is a place to sit and trail your hands or dip your feet in the water, and to create mystery, a stretch where there's no access to the water.

An island of rock creates a natural focal point in a pond. Choose a boulder that has a fine silhouette and an interesting surface, because both will show clearly in its reflection. Treetops and tall reeds also cast beautiful reflections. The flowering quince *(Chaenomeles)* ensures that you stop here and notice these details.

A free-form or kidney-shaped pool is not easy to fit into a garden naturally, especially on flat land and close to the straight lines of a house. Two simple ways of integrating it well are shown here: the shape of the pool is echoed in the shapes of the lawn and paths around it, and where the pool turns, it turns for a reason, around an outcropping of boulders, so the curves don't seem so arbitrary.

Landscape architect: Thomas Church

Make one side of a pool inaccessible with a low stone wall and natural plantings.

Boulders and plants loosen up a flagstone terrace around a rectangular pool. The large boulder in the background helps to shelter the seats. Low boulders double as places to sit or dive into the water.

Design: Heide Stolpestad Baldwin

A rockery forms part of the edge of this pond. The stones and the plants growing in the crevices are reflected on the water surface. Below the surface, mysterious among the water weeds, are more rocks, partially covered in silt. The lantern on the promontory is a snow-viewing *(yukimi)* lantern — its broad hat is designed to collect a beautiful dome of snow.

Ringing a pond with a necklace of stone can look artificial. Prevent that by using large, irregularly shaped pieces of stone and be sure to use the same stone elsewhere in the garden — to edge a path and make a wall or waterfall.

Water-washed slabs of stone form a bridge that allows you to walk over the pond within an inch or two of the water surface. Stones with placid shapes, reclining or horizontal, look particularly beautiful with still water.

FOUNTAINS

The sound of water splashing from a fountain brings a garden to life. In a sunny part of the garden, the spray also cools the air and sparkles in the sunlight. Choose a spot out of the wind, so that the water doesn't fly away in the air, or install a stone fountain that is attractive when the water is turned off.

In a hot courtyard garden, moving water cools the air and provides a pretty focal point. This fountain was carved from the same Mexican stone as the cut stone bricks that edge the catchment pond and the rill. The gravel, from a local source, complements the color of the imported stone.

Landscape architect: Jonathan Plant & Associates

Insert a faucet or a metal pipe for a waterspout while you are constructing a wall. You'll also need a hole lower in the wall to run the tubing from the fountain pump in the trough to the waterspout.

Water can be made to spill in a symphony of different sounds. From the bamboo pipe here, water splashes onto the boulder, ripples over its surface, sheets and tips and drips off into the pool, then gushes over the lip of the pool to the stream below. The sounds are magnified by the walls of rock and the foliage around the water.

A series of circles—geometry at its softest—provides the necessary sense of grandeur around this statue fountain. The stone figure sits at the center of a circular pond (the fountain pump is hidden in the stone plinth). The stone pond sits within a circle of pinks *(Dianthus),* and the pinks sit within a circle of rough stone.

A bamboo pipe drips water slowly into an almost still reflection of the sky. Situated at the edge of a path heading uphill through trees, the fountain dripping and the light on the water surface stop you in your tracks, just where you might notice a fallen tree trunk covered in emerald moss.

The water bubbling from a fountainhead inside a boulder and cascading down its sides stains the stone with a watermark and sends soothing sounds across the patio. Even the relatively soft sound of water from a small fountain will distract the ear from traffic noise.

Design: Suzanne Edison

WATER BOWLS

A circle of water in a bowl pulls a piece of sky down to the ground. In the very smallest garden, you can watch the clouds passing over and the wind rippling on the water. Place water bowls to stop people where there's something special to see, or put them at the intersections of paths, the tops of steps, or on a patio to put a little punch into the design.

To make a Japanese *tsukubai* (handwashing station), arrange a natural boulder next to a stone bowl so that you can sit or squat and wash your hands there.

Some boulders have natural dimples that collect rainwater after a storm. If you are lucky enough to find one, site it so that the water can be seen from a path or patio. Alternatively, buy a boulder that has been carved to collect water; if you look closely you may notice that one edge of the boulder has been dammed with rock-colored cement. The boulder above sits at the top of the steps from the house to the swimming pool. The boulder at right sits at the edge of a patio. Both gardens have several other boulders of the same type of rock in the vicinity.

Design, top: Heide Stolpestad Baldwin

Design, right: The Berger Partnership

Settled into a bed of golden star *(Chrysogonum virginianum),* which flowers from spring on and off through fall, this quiet eye of water in a block of stone is certain to be discovered. The pattern of the leaves of an overhanging tree appears silhouetted against the sky.

A concrete base raises this carved granite water bowl clear of the grass, so that its fine silhouette is clearly visible. Japanese stone water basins *(chozubachi)* are often raised on slabs of stone.

Design: Tom Chakas

Flickering light falling through treetops dances like diamonds across dark water in the shade. This basin draws you off the path and brings you by a pretty Dutchman's breeches *(Dicentra cucullaria),* which deserves to be seen up close.

A stone sculpture collects a lake of water that mirrors the surrounding plantings. The water is high enough off the ground that you can trail your fingers through it. It's also shallow enough for birds to bathe in it when you're not near.

Sculpture: Welton Rotz

Dry Creekbeds

Dry creekbeds suggest water. Some do it with realistic-looking steep banks, steps for the water to slip over, and different sizes of river rock—from boulders to smooth gravel—arranged on the stream floor the way the forces of nature might have deposited them there. Others take the poetic line of flowing water and stylize it, with one or two sizes of pebbles standing in for the water.

A river of pebbles and rocks slips down the slope between banks planted with carpet bugle *(Ajuga)* and sedum ground covers, and clumps of irises and lily-of-the-Nile *(Agapanthus)*. The boulder step in the stream is a particularly authentic-looking detail. A lily-of-the-Nile holds the lower bank firm there, so water must leap over the stone.

Design: Roy and Erlda Young

Water collects here in a marsh of sea lavender *(Limonium perezii)*, murmurs downhill around boulders, and disappears under a dramatic clump of wachendorfia into a grove of bamboo. In a breeze, the bamboo foliage and the sea lavender flowers shiver over the blue-gray stones, creating rippling shadows like the movement of water. Other elements in the garden—the lawn and the flower beds— swing in symphony with the lines of the swale.

Design: Stephanie Kotin and Christopher Tebbutt, Land & Place

Think water: take the dry stream around a promontory and past a beach downstream, and place a stepping-stone midstream for the tantalizing chance to leave shore.

A wash of river rock running through the lowest point in the garden emphasizes the contours of the land. The banks and bluffs overlooking the wash can be sculpted and a secluded sitting place on a boulder made behind the trees. Note the scale of the river rock and how jumbled it is; you can almost hear the torrent of water that surely races through here after a storm. In dry climates, rainwater can be harvested in a wash and sent downhill to plants that need it.

Stepping-stones *(left)* over a gravel streambed conjure the image of water lapping at their sides, especially if the stones are too large to be swept away by the water. A stone slab *(right)* takes a stepping-stone path across the flood to a viewing place at the water's edge. Note the boulders anchoring the bridge at each side — a traditional Japanese garden detail — and the boulder stranded midstream. A hefty wooden bridge with square metal insets *(below)* is anchored to the bank with a collection of boulders and pebbles.

Design, above left: Matsutani and Associates
Design, below: Steve Walker

A stylized dry water course swings out from under trees through a conventional mowed lawn, creating a playful pale line across a bright green canvas (and tying together two different areas of the garden). At first glance, the eye takes in the shape of the pebbled rill; looking again, the rill becomes negative space between the looping, almost organic, shapes of the lawn.

A bed of gravel and pebbles flowing like water makes a strikingly decorative natural line and pattern against the periwinkle *(Vinca)* banks. Pools and streams of gravel are a useful ground cover in oak woodland, which shouldn't be disturbed with garden irrigation.

To make a Japanese-style dry waterfall *(karetaki),* arrange the rocks so that the water travels deep within a gorge, and choose a stone with a flat face for the falls.

At the head of this dry stream is a quiet sitting place and an intriguing *shishi-odoshi* (deer chaser) bamboo fountain that calls you up the path. The long piece of bamboo is pivoted on the bamboo post; as water pours through it, it tips and knocks loudly against the boulder in the stream, and the sound is amplified by the hillside.

Tall banks help make the course of the creek seem perfectly natural and inevitable. A strong outside edge where the creek swings around a bend stops the water from running directly downhill. Note the boulders stranded in midstream, too heavy for the current to move.

Landscape architect: Owen Dell

A dry creek bubbles out of the mountains—denoted by a towering boulder with a majestic presence and dark boulders tumbled at its feet—into the lowlands, where pale, smooth, reclining boulders form a promontory and a gorge for the stream to flow by and through. A fish sculpture adds to the sense of play.

STREAMS AND WATERFALLS

Small waterfalls and streams are often the most natural looking and sound the most soothing. Even a little waterfall—nothing more than a single step—in a stream will set the water chuckling loudly so that the sound carries farther into the garden.

A Japanese maple *(Acer palmatum)* lends some extra height and drama to a series of low falls. It also decorates the pools and rocks with flurries of bright autumn leaves and casts a beautiful reflection on the still water of the pond.

Bridge a stream with a slab of natural stone, and arrange boulders at each of the corners.

At the edge of a still pond that reflects the surrounding grasses and trees, a small waterfall spills over a rock, making a pleasant, gentle splash and a few ripples. The fall is tucked into mounding grasses, which substitute for a natural bank.

Design: Conni Cross

The sound of a small stream can draw people toward it from across the garden even when there's no view of water. Make the sound musical by installing occasional steps in the floor of the water channel so that the water skips and splashes, and amplify the sounds by making the sides to the water channel deep. The banks of the stream pictured below are planted with English lavender *(Lavandula angustifolia)*, society garlic *(Tulbaghia violacea)*, blue oat grass *(Helictotrichon sempervirens)*, and Mexican evening primrose *(Oenothera speciosa)*. Bougainvillea 'Rosenka' arches over the stream pictured at left.

ABOVE AND RIGHT: Making parts of a stream inaccessible or hiding the stream between steep banks generates a sense of adventure. The imagination hunts for a trail to the bank or ponders on what lies beyond the bend.

ROCK GARDENS

In Victorian times, rock gardeners wouldn't have considered a new tulip a proper plant for a rock garden. They planted only true alpines in their gardens and arranged the stones in hillocks to mimic windswept mountain ranges. Today, anything goes when it comes to combining stone and plants.

A rock garden may look like a meadow, with grasses or wild-flowers growing there. Rockeries are built in woodland gardens, with violets and moss thriving among the boulders in the shade; and they are in desert gardens, where vivid-colored cacti flowers bloom against the buff-colored rock. A modern rock garden influenced by Japanese gardening might be almost all stone—patterns of cut stone and natural stone laid out on gravel, or boulders set into raked oceans of sand. All of these gardens are shown in the following pages, plus the smallest rock gardens of all—a boulder used as a garden accent and a portable stone trough that can be placed anywhere in a garden.

If your aim is to suggest a large scene from nature, such as a mountain range, site the rock garden carefully. Place it away from the house, the lawn, and any large-leafed shrubs and trees that might reveal the deception in scale you are trying to achieve. Use gravel paths and terraces, or stony meadows, at the edges of the rock garden to help create a transition between the rock garden and the rest of the garden. Or copy the solution found in Japanese dry gardens and place the rock garden in its own space surrounded by a hedge or a plain fence.

Small- or delicate-featured plants will help preserve a miniaturized scale. You might choose as wide a selection as you can fit into the rock garden (you can tailor the soil in each crevice to suit your plants), or you might follow nature and let one or two plants predominate, forming fields and valleys of a single color. Some of the more visually interesting rock gardens are collections of the myriad forms of one species—gardens consisting of almost all houseleeks *(Sempervivum),* for example, or stonecrops *(Sedum);* the stone can then be chosen to complement the dominant colors.

A huge variety of plants can look fussy and busy; to establish some calm, perhaps choose plants with just pink or yellow flowers (or any other pair of colors) for the peak flower season. Trough gardens are another solution if you'd like to house a large collection of plants: have as much variety as you like by creating many tiny, separate rock gardens.

You'll see in the following pages that a few large stones make more impact than many small ones. One stone can have enough presence to be the center of the garden. Choose a boulder for its naturalness, its straightforward, unassumingly beautiful lines. If you are making a composition of several boulders, vary the sizes so that some are dominant and some subordinate and vary the distance between the boulders, but choose just one kind of stone.

Bands of pebbles and cobbles, some set on edge, some set flat, swirl through this garden floor, generating a lively, playful atmosphere in a small space.

Design: Jeff Bale

More important than the interesting surface or shape of a boulder is its look of stability and permanence. This is most easily generated by burying the stone to its widest point. At the stone yard, assess how much a boulder will need to be buried before you buy it.

Design: Harry Carle Everett

Instead of traditional boxwood hedges, cut slabs of Pennsylvania bluestone mark out this formal knot garden. The stone slabs are 10 inches wide and 7 inches thick. Between them grow rock garden plants such as stonecrops *(Sedum)* and species bulbs that appreciate the warmth given off by the stones.

Design: Dan Borroff Landscape

A fan of small natural stepping-stones set deeply into the lawn marks the approach to a traditional Japanese standing lantern *(tachi doro)*.

A giant spire of stone among conifers suggests a mountain landscape at nature photographer Art Wolfe's garden in Seattle.

SLOPES AND ROCKERIES

Classic rock gardens of gemlike alpine plants have become few and far between. The new rockery combines stone with almost any type of plant, as long as it is relatively delicate in scale.

Make a ledge garden by setting stone slabs firmly into the face of a slope. To mask the gap between two small slabs, place a mat-forming plant there.

A composition of two-fifths rock and three-fifths plants is considered ideal for a rock garden, or rockery. Too much rock and the garden can look stark; too little and the garden doesn't hold together visually. Most alpines bloom in late spring or summer; here, in the foreground, are rock jasmine *(Androsace lanuginosa)*, common thrift *(Armeria maritima),* and pink *(Dianthus).*

In natural meadows, the plant and rock palette is not usually diverse, or at least not obviously so. One kind of grass or one or two wildflowers predominate, seeding themselves across the ground, and the stone is usually of the same type. Copying that repetition helps to achieve a natural effect in the garden. Repeated clumps of bold-textured phormiums unify the meadow pictured at right. Houseleeks *(Sempervivum)* create a rhythmic pattern on the slope pictured below.

True alpine plants often thrive in crevices. The drainage and the air circulation around the plant's crown are excellent, and the rocks keep the plant roots cool in hot weather. In the natural outcropping of rock pictured above, pale yellow basket-of-gold *(Aurinia saxatilis* 'Citrina'), columbine *(Aquilegia canadensis),* and *Schivereckia podolica* grow among the rocks. Geraniums and violets spill from the crevice pictured above right; this crevice was made by placing two boulders closely together.

Design, above right: Harland Hand

Slate is one of the ground covers in these terraces, which zigzag down a steep hillside garden in droughty southern California. Seen from the house, high above, the color and texture of the stone stand out well among the clumps of blue and purple grasses, and fields of hen and chicks *(Echeveria elegans)* and snow-in-summer *(Cerastium tomentosum).*

Landscape architect: Isabelle Greene & Associates

A plant's form is sometimes particularly well matched to the form of the rocks. For example, a mounding stonecrop *(Sedum kamtschaticum),* right, pours over rounded boulders; a spidery, prostrate broom *(Genista pilosa),* below, sprawls across a flat-topped boulder.

Make a rock outcropping on a flat site by mounding soil into a berm and placing jagged rocks onto the face of it so that they seem to have been forced upward out of the bedrock.

A stepped rockery built like a series of stone raised beds provides seating and paths among the flowers. Growing here are sunrose *(Helianthemum nummularium),* potentilla, iris, thrift *(Armeria),* stonecrop *(Sedum),* campanulas, Alpine poppy *(Papaver alpinum),* rockcress *(Arabis),* speedwell *(Veronica),* and evening primrose *(Oenothera macrocarpa).*

Moisture- and shade-loving plants—primrose, astilbe, ferns, monkey flower *(Mimulus),* and water plantain *(Plantago major* 'Atropurpurea') — grow in the crevices of these magnificent rocks by the water. Note the balance among water, rock, and plants.

Design: Eryl Morton

Rock gardens seem most natural when sited near other stone features—a stone house or wall, stone troughs, or gravel paths and patios. A low-growing, wide-spreading yellow broom *(Genista pilosa)* is the centerpiece of the rock garden above. Saxifrage, iris, and magenta *Geranium cinereum subcaulescens* are the highlights in the garden at right.

Container Gardens

English stone sinks and water troughs made ideal containers for miniature rock gardens a century ago, when they were cheap and plentiful. The contemporary trough gardener uses a wide range of containers, including inexpensive and rugged looking hypertufa pots.

A hypertufa pot made of cement, peat moss, and vermiculite (see page 109) is a fair replica of true stone. The front bowl contains *Lewisia cotyledon* set in a circle of stonecrop *(Sedum album* 'Murale'). The larger bowl holds Florida heather *(Cuphea hyssopifolia)*, sweet alyssum *(Lobularia maritima)*, and Mexican feather grass *(Stipa tenuissima)*.

Place a trough on a flat-topped boulder or a pile of rocks to bring delicately scaled plants closer to eye level.

A stack of flues and a series of round, black dish containers provide some height in this exciting collection of succulents. The unifying element among so much color and textural variety is the mulch of brick-colored gravel, which is spread on the ground and in the containers.

Design: Archie Days

A stone trough on stone pillars sits on an apron of gravel at the edge of a cut stone walkway. The gray-leaved licorice plant *(Helichrysum petiolare)* and bright fuchsia and geraniums *(Pelargonium)* stand out crisply and elegantly against the dark green yew *(Taxus)* hedge behind.

A metal wagon with rock garden plants is parked on a gravel path against a stone wall, a properly stony environment. In cold-winter regions, a mobile rock garden container can be towed into a sheltered spot until spring; in areas with hot summers, sensitive plants can be moved into the shade.

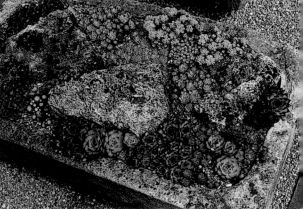

A silvery green stonecrop *(Sedum)* with yellow flowers sits on the edge of a trough of various houseleeks *(Sempervivum)*. There are hundreds of varieties of stonecrops and houseleeks. The contrasting colors, textures, and forms of either genus can make a striking trough display. Note the equally interesting texture of the stones and the way they separate the trough into different growing fields.

Any small plant with a delicate scale, not just alpines, suits a trough garden. Here, on a mossy bank are violas planted with *Iris cristata* and English daisies *(Bellis)*.

BOULDERS AS ACCENTS

A Japanese-style garden may be centered around a single stone chosen for the personality suggested in its lines and shape. The goal is usually to place a boulder naturally, to make it look as if it's always been there. Use moss and fine-textured plants to help anchor a boulder and also to give a grouping of boulders coherence.

In nature, stone is frequently strewn about chaotically, with none of the order that the human eye finds satisfying. A natural-looking arrangement of stones in a garden actually has some order to it. The stones have been chosen for their variety in size and arranged dynamically. Moss is excellent for unifying stone compositions.

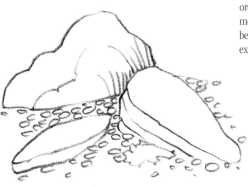

To make a composition around a large rounded rock, choose a reclining rock and a flat rock— all their shapes are placid and peaceful.

The heft and solidity of stone are best set off by plants with graceful foliage, such as grasses and ferns. In keeping with the Japanese garden style, this American garden contains mostly foliage plants and relatively few flowers.

Design: The Berger Partnership

A stone sculpture by Welton Rotz makes a focal point and a sitting place in this colorful flower garden. The massiveness of the stone contrasts with the fragility of the flowers, but there's a sense of balance: neither overwhelms the other.

In a Japanese garden, the major stones suggest things beyond themselves. An upright stone might symbolize a mountain, a guardian deity, or a monk in his robes. A stone is chosen for its personality; its lines and shape must touch the imagination.

A specimen rock in a Chinese-style garden is not chosen for its naturalness but for its eccentricity. The most favored rocks — usually of limestone eroded by water — are the tallest, most fantastically contorted ones with the most holes.

Loops of gravel and groups of boulders draw your eye into this oak woodland on a slope above the house. The pattern is attractive from the house entrance and from the rooms indoors. If you choose to explore, the gravel offers a path across the hillside, in and out of the dappled light, to the hilltop where there's a view. The boulders provide places to stop and rest along the way.

Landscape architect: Van Atta Associates

73

Granite boulders and cacti bring the scale and drama of the surrounding desert into the garden, over the patio wall, and right up to the house. Desert stone can be exceptionally warm and pretty in color; it looks best in the context of piercing sun and vividly colored cacti blooms. In regions with softer light, it may seem strident and out of place.

Bring small rocks into better relationship with one another by placing them on an island of gravel, moss, or fine-textured ground cover.

Carved, sleeping stone heads and ceramic devil faces have surfaced on this gravely bank among natural boulders and pebbles with pink, purple, and rust colored faces. The distinctions between natural and unnatural, animate and inanimate, are interestingly blurred.

Design: Keeyla Meadows. Sculpture: Marcia Donahue (stone), Keeyla Meadows (ceramic)

Three standing stones, with distinct shapes, sizes, and personalities, provide children with something to climb on and places to hide or play in the shade. Aesthetically, they fit into the garden much more easily than manufactured play equipment.

Boulders with strong individual character sit at the corner of a swimming pool, their shapes and colors reflected in the water. The formal positioning of the boulders and the informal planting around them help marry the geometric pool to its natural surroundings.

Design: Heide Stolpestad Baldwin

Asymmetrical balance is the key to arranging boulders in the Japanese style. The main stone, also called the guardian stone or host stone, establishes the center of the composition. It is mountainous—serene, solid, and immortal looking. The side mountain slightly in front of the main stone makes the main stone look farther away, and therefore bigger.

Landscape architect: Isabelle Greene & Associates

GRAVEL GARDENS

A gravel garden floor provides a simple open space. You can make exquisite natural scenery there with a few rocks, evergreen trees or shrubs, or rhythmic lines of stepping-stones. With the addition of some raked waves, the gravel becomes an infinite-seeming sea.

The ripples in Japanese sand gardens suggest water. They often follow the outlines of the stones, circling each stone or bringing two or three stones together on an island. The sand used is actually more like gravel; the particles may be almost half an inch across. Because the glare is too great from white gravel, use gray or tan-colored gravel, or mix the white with mica or a dark gravel to minimize its brightness; some people use turkey grit from an agricultural supplier. Wet the gravel, tamp it flat, then pull the rake through the gravel toward you. When you're done, set your waves with a fine spray.

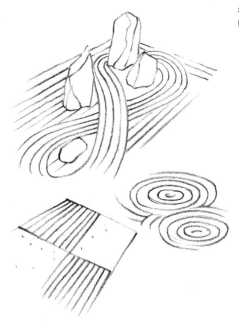

Try raking checkerboard or eddy patterns through a sand garden, or loop the loop around archipelagos of small stones. A Japanese rake would be useful.

A floor of gravel bounded by evergreen hedges is the simple stage on which classical Japanese gardeners arranged boulders to generate flights of imagination. There could be no better setting for this stone sculpture by Richard Long.

Design: Pamela Burton

A Japanese garden is essentially simple and spare. The shrubs and trees are usually evergreen and spaced openly; some are pruned to control the space they occupy. The proportions of all things—stones, leaves, flowers, trees, and shrubs—are related so that nothing breaks up the harmony. The stones have an unassuming beauty; they don't dominate the scene. Although the garden is often small, it contains a great sense of space and endless time.

Japanese gardens place great importance on the ground plane. Here, three different types of paving—stepping-stones, angular cut stone in irregular bands, and natural stones in straight bands—mark out a series of spaces within a gravel garden. The different forms and natural colors of the stone and the raked patterns in the gravel serve as the garden scenery.

There's a sense of calm in both of these Japanese-inspired western gardens. The granite parterre above balances space and mass, presents the timeless-ness of stone alongside trimmed squares of burgeoning green. The informal garden at left also has that signature Japanese balance of stone and green-ery; the natural rock outcropping makes treasured scenery.

Design, above: Hiroshi Nanmori

A GUIDE TO CONSTRUCTION

Working with stone is an ancient activity: since the first fields were tilled, stones have been collected from the earth and turned into simple paths, walls, and mosaics. Today it's still slow, patient work for the most part, but it is also very rewarding work, because of the natural beauty of the material and the sense of crafting something permanent.

This chapter explains the basic techniques for building with stone. It includes detailed information on installing stone paths and patios—in a rustic or elegant style—as well as stone steps, simple dry-stone walls with places for plants, pebble and bamboo fountains, authentic-looking dry creekbeds, and rock gardens on rock slabs and screes and Japanese-style mounds. Although some fine stonework requires years of training, these projects are relatively simple ones that you can do yourself.

Start out with the right tools for the job and suitable stone (see "A Guide to Shopping," pages 110–127). The more efficiently and pleasingly your project swings along, the more you'll enjoy working with stone.

A stone retaining wall less than 3 feet high is a feasible project if you work slowly.

BEFORE YOU BEGIN

Clearing weeds, seeing to drainage and grading, excavating, and making a proper foundation are all preliminary tasks that may be essential for a successful project. Before you begin, also take the time to think about safety: your safety while you are building and the safety of the finished project.

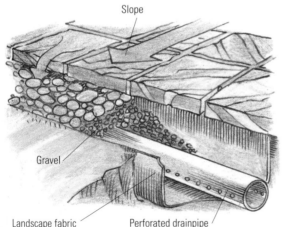

Slope

Gravel

Landscape fabric

Perforated drainpipe

CLEARING WEEDS

Clear the ground of weeds and weed seeds before you start building. Use synthetic herbicides only as a last resort when all other methods fail. Apart from the risks they may pose to health and the environment, many of these chemicals can damage desirable plants if they drift through the air or run off in irrigation or rainwater (if the damage is to a neighboring property, bear in mind that you can be held responsible). Some persist in the soil for long periods, injuring later plantings. If you use herbicides, make sure the product is at least safe for nearby plants.

The easier and simpler option is to pull or dig out the weeds, hoe them, or rototill or disc them. Try to get to weeds before they seed, and remove every piece of perennial weeds that have thick taproots or creeping root systems. Weed the site every few weeks for a while, watering after each weeding to encourage any remaining dormant seeds or root fragments to sprout.

Laying landscape fabric (made of woven or spun synthetic materials) can help suppress weeds. Many gardeners use it in paving projects, especially under gravel paths and patios. The density and porosity of the fabric vary with the manufacturer; the denser fabrics are better for suppressing weeds, but the fabric must be permeable or the path or patio may flood.

DRAINAGE AND GRADING

Whenever you pave an area, its drainage is affected, because water tends to run off even the most porous paving. The natural drainage of the site is also affected when you put a large solid object, such as a concrete retaining wall or a pond, in the soil.

Unless the site slopes naturally, grade before paving so that runoff won't collect where it can cause problems—against a house foundation, for example. Allow a pitch of at least 1 inch in 8 feet (or $1/8$ inch per foot). Pay particular attention to grading a large area of impermeable paving; gravel paths on a bed of sand probably don't need too much attention.

To draw off water from the edge of a graded area, place perforated plastic drainpipe in a bed of gravel, as shown. Dig a trench about 12 inches deep (deeper if the ground freezes), and line it with landscape fabric to prevent soil from clogging the pipe. Lay the pipe, perforated side down, in the trench, and pack gravel around it to a depth of 6 inches.

Perforated drainpipe in a gravel trench is also the simplest way of drawing off water that will collect behind a retaining wall or a pond. If you neglect to lay the pipe, the pressure of the accumulated soil water could burst the wall or pop the pond out of the ground. Ponds most at risk are those at the base of a slope.

EXCAVATING

Many stone projects require excavations for foundation and drainage materials. A simple way to excavate to the correct depth across a wide area is to lay out twine between stakes and take your measurements from the twine as you dig. Any adjustments for grading can be incorporated. The directions that follow are for patios, but they'll work for any project.

Drive stakes into the ground a few inches beyond the patio corners, as shown on the next page. Mark the desired patio level on one stake for reference. Attach a length of twine to that stake, set the twine at the mark, and stretch it toward the adjacent stake. Tie the twine to the second stake and use a line level (a small tool that clips onto the line) to make the twine level. Continue to the third and fourth stakes, adjusting the twine to ensure that it's level, and marking each stake where the twine crosses it.

For an entirely flat project, with no allowance for drainage (see preceding page), you could excavate from these lines, measuring down a distance equal to the thickness of your paving material plus the thickness of the foundation materials or setting bed. To pitch the surface slightly so that rainwater runs off it, make the following adjustments in the twine: Calculate the total drop in level required (1 inch for every 8 feet) and mark this below the level marks on the downslope stakes, as shown at right. Restring the twine to these new marks. Now if you measure down from the twine and excavate to a depth equal to the thickness of the paving and foundation materials, you'll be building in the pitch.

Before you begin excavating, be sure that your lines are square by measuring the distance between diagonals, as shown above right. They should be equal. If the paved surface adjoins a house or other structure, leave a small gap so that you can install galvanized metal flashing to protect wood siding or floor framing from moisture damage.

For a large area, the twine lines around the perimeter may not be enough to use as reference points for excavating. In that case, add more lines of twine and stakes to make 5-foot squares.

Excavate carefully, with the goal of laying the foundation materials on firm, undisturbed soil. If you dig too deep you'll need to fill, and fill will inevitably settle, taking your paving with it. If you find yourself with a low spot, fill it with decomposed granite (d.g.); even the d.g. with a rake, moisten it, then tamp it several times with a hand tamper or a rented power vibrator.

PATH AND PATIO FOUNDATIONS

No matter which stone paving you choose, you will probably have to prepare a foundation, or subbase. Although it's heavy work pouring gravel and sand or concrete, don't skimp on the construction, or the paving may buckle and sink. For large areas, equip yourself with back-saving tools (a sturdy wheelbarrow is a must) or consider having a contractor lay the foundation materials for you.

The foundation needs to be particularly deep if your soil is unstable—for example, if it floods, cracks badly in summer, or heaves from frost. As you plan your path or patio, bear in mind that small, thin paving units are more likely to be sent askew by movement in the soil than large slabs of stone six inches thick.

SAFETY ABOVE ALL ELSE

Working with stone is rewarding, but it is sometimes heavy work. Take precautions so that you don't injure yourself. Wear sturdy boots and gloves when you're transporting heavy materials, and

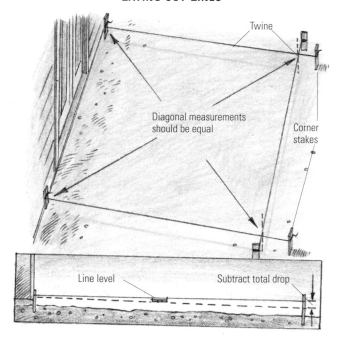

LAYING OUT LINES

Twine

Diagonal measurements should be equal

Corner stakes

Line level

Subtract total drop

EXCAVATING FOR A WIDE AREA

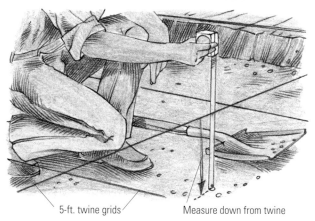

5-ft. twine grids

Measure down from twine

keep out of the way of a stone that might roll or a wheelbarrow or cart that might tip. On slopes, always start work from the base and embed each stone firmly before bringing the next into place. Don't bite off more than you can chew: start out with the right equipment for the work and, if necessary, make it a team project, enlisting the help of a friend and perhaps a contractor.

It's also important to build well, so that the finished project doesn't pose a safety hazard. Consult your local building department about codes as necessary. Hire a landscape architect or an engineer if your site has drainage or erosion problems or you're building on a steep slope or on fill. As you plan, imagine the finished project: Will children rush to the water's edge? Will the path be used after dark? Are the steps comfortable for people of all ages? Be smart and figure these things out before you begin.

STEPPING-STONES

Stepping-stones are fun and easy to lay. Arrange them differently in different areas of the garden—spaced generously to quicken people's pace through a storage area or laid closely together to slow people down to smell the roses. Raise the stones above grade to show them off and keep them clear of litter, or set them flush in a lawn so the lawn mower cruises over them without snagging. Whichever options you choose, be sure to create a path full of swing.

CHOOSING YOUR PACE

Large gaps between stepping-stones encourage people to gallop along; small gaps slow people down. On a functional path, for example, between the back door and the compost pile, gaps of 10 to 12 inches are appropriate—there's probably no reason for lingering. For a leisurely tour through an ornamental part of the garden, make the gaps much smaller, from 4 to 6 inches between stones.

The larger the gaps, the larger the stones should be in order to look good and provide sure footing to someone hurrying from point A to point B. If you are building a path for a slower pace, you can use smaller stones (but don't choose stones less than 18 inches long, because the path won't seem gracious and inviting), and you can use stones with less even surfaces.

LAYING STEPPING-STONES IN SOIL

Stepping-stones in flower or vegetable gardens or woodland are best laid so that they sit 1 or 2 inches above grade. Water will drain off raised stones, and surrounding soil and fallen leaves won't wash onto them. They are also displayed more handsomely set above grade.

LAYING STEPPING-STONES IN LAWN

Stepping-stone paths across lawn are often laid flush with the soil, for convenience. You can run the mower right over the stones, even on the tightest cut, if you lay them flush. If you lay the stones raised, you'll need to trim the grass around each stone by hand.

Once you've cut around each stone with a straight-edged spade, peel off the turf with the blade of the spade, and excavate to the full depth of the stone plus 1 inch. Spread 1 inch of sand in the hole, and settle the stone into the sand until it's flat and firm and flush with the soil surface.

LAYING STEPPING-STONES IN SOIL

1 Lay out the stepping-stones on top of the soil in a pleasing line. Arrange them so that the spaces between them provide a comfortable, regular pace.

2 Cut around each stone with a spade (or a knife) to mark its shape, and then move the stone to one side.

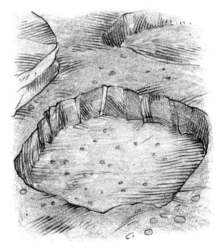

3 Excavate a hole for the stone with a straight-edged spade. Make it half as deep as the thickness of the stone plus 1 inch; for example, if the stone is 4 inches thick, dig the hole 3 inches deep (the stone will sit on a 1-inch sand base and rise 2 inches above grade).

Laying stepping-stones in gravel

Laying stepping-stones raised above surrounding gravel will help keep the gravel from skittering over the stones. In an existing gravel path or patio, excavate holes for the stones

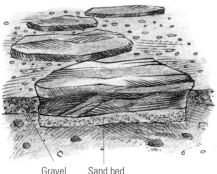

Gravel   Sand bed

and lay them as you would if you were laying them in soil as described on the preceding page. If you are starting the path or patio from scratch, lay the landscape fabric, install the sand or decomposed granite base, then settle the stepping-stones on the base before spreading the gravel. Be sure to buy stepping-stones that are at least 3 inches thick, so they will protrude above the minimum 2-inch layer of gravel.

A note about foundations

A 1-inch-thick sand base is sufficient for most stepping-stones in most situations. In cold-winter climates or poorly drained soils, install 4 to 8 inches of gravel below the sand; see page 81 for more information on foundations. Be especially careful to make a proper base if the path is used regularly throughout the year in all weathers and light conditions. You don't want to be continually checking stones and resettling any wobbling ones to keep the path safe. On sloping sites, consider setting the stones in mortar; see pages 89 and 95 for more information on using mortar.

Large, heavy stepping-stones obviously don't get dislodged as easily as small, thin ones. In fact, if your stones are large and sturdy and your soil conditions stable, you can lay stepping-stones directly on the soil, without a base.

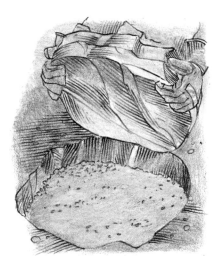

4 Spread 1 inch of sand in the hole, and wet it with a fine spray. Place the stone in the hole and twist it into the sand, until the stone is level and firm.

5 Add more sand around and beneath the stone if necessary, and water the sand to finish settling the stone.

SWINGING ALONG

A straight stepping-stone path made of uniform pavers laid one behind the other has little charm compared to this irregular path designed by landscape architect Ron Herman.

The boulder at the corner draws the eye and invites you to see what's around the corner. The two "threshold stones" at the beginning of the path are also eye-catching and inviting—and large enough to linger on before you start out into the garden.

Set up a pleasing rhythm in the shape of the path by aligning the stones off center and swinging the line of the path out around any shrub or tree or rock outcropping along the way. Place the longest sides of the stones so that they lie across the path and the steps are more broad than deep, like a staircase. Whenever possible, lay the stones so that the shapes speak to one another—a concave edge of one stone laid against a convex edge of another.

Raising the stones above a sea of pebbles evokes a pleasant feeling of crossing over, and it keeps the pebbles from spilling over the stones.

GRAVEL

Gravel—either smooth river rock that rolls underfoot or the more stable, mechanically crushed rock—makes a low-cost, fast-draining path or patio surface. Edge it to keep it from spreading into the rest of the garden, and lay it on a sand base so that it feels firm underfoot.

INSTALLING EDGINGS

Unless gravel is contained within edgings, it tends to travel into adjoining areas of the garden, leaving behind a sunken, uneven surface and bare spots where the underlying landscape fabric shows. For straight-edged paths and patios, the most popular edgings are made of 2-by-6 lumber; choose pressure-treated lumber or the heartwood of cedar, redwood, or certain types of cypress. For curves, use flexible redwood benderboard or sturdy recycled plastic edgings.

To start, dig out the area to be paved to a depth of 3 inches—assuming 1 inch of base material, 2 inches of gravel. String twine to mark the path or patio perimeter and the height of the edging boards, 1 inch above the finished gravel surface (see page 81).

BENDERBOARD CURVES

Soak wooden benderboard in water to make it more flexible. Then work it around stakes set on the inside edge of the curve, nailing or screwing the board to these stakes. For the outside curve of a path or patio, add stakes every 3 feet or so on the outside and fasten the benderboard to them; then pull up the temporary inside stakes so that there are no stakes within the path or patio perimeter. Bend additional boards around the first board, staggering any splices, until you've built up the curved edging to the same thickness as the straight sections. Nail all layers together between the stakes.

Outside curve · Temporary inner stakes removed once board is secured · Permanent stakes · Inside curve

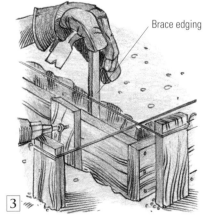

Brace edging

INSTALLING EDGINGS

1. Make a narrow trench below the marked perimeter lines to accommodate the edging. The top edge of the lumber should just touch the twine.

2. Working on the outside of the perimeter lines, drive in 1-by-3 or 2-by-2 stakes flush with the lines. Place one stake at each side of a corner, at each joint where two boards meet, and at intervals of 4 feet along each length of board.

3. After fastening the edging boards together, place them in the trench, and attach them to the stakes with nails or screws as shown.

4. Saw off the exposed sections of the stakes at an angle; then pack the excavated soil to fill in around the outside of the edging.

LANDSCAPE FABRIC AND WEEDS

It's common practice to lay landscape fabric over the excavated ground before laying the sand base and gravel surface. The fabric provides a barrier to weeds that might otherwise grow up from the soil through the sand and gravel. However, landscape fabric isn't magic. Weed seeds that fall onto the surface of the gravel often germinate in it, so you will need to weed the gravel occasionally anyway. If you lay fabric, be sure it is permeable so that rainwater drains through it, off the path or patio surface. If you choose not to lay fabric, weed the area, water it to encourage remaining seeds to sprout, and reweed several times before laying the base materials.

LAYING THE SAND BASE

Gravel surfaces tend to shift when walked on, but the movement will be minimized if you lay a compacted base of sand. For large areas, consider renting a drum roller to compact the materials, or, even better, a power vibrator.

STRONG EDGINGS AND SOFT

Edgings are necessary to contain the gravel, but they need not be dull. A path may be bounded by striking black, curved, rubber edgings, as shown above right, to accentuate the shape of the path and highlight the contrasts in color and texture between path and garden. Or, the edging can be made invisible, a simple strip of metal, hard plastic, or wood that becomes lost beneath soft plantings and promontories of boulders, as shown below right.

You can make a feature of the edging (top) or hide it (bottom).

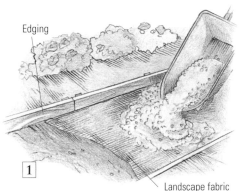

Edging

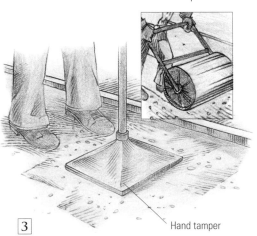

Landscape fabric

LAYING A GRAVEL PATH

1. Install the edgings first, then put down landscape fabric if you like, to help protect against weeds. Pour sand or decomposed granite (d.g.) over the site, taking care not to dislodge the landscape fabric.

2. Rake the sand or d.g. evenly until it is a uniform 1-inch thickness. As you rake, wet the material with a fine spray.

3. Using a drum roller or hand tamper, pass over the wet base several times, packing it down firmly.

4. Spread the gravel at least 2 inches thick and rake it evenly over the base. Using the roller or tamper, press the gravel into place (the rolling will also help turn the sharp edges down).

Spray nozzle

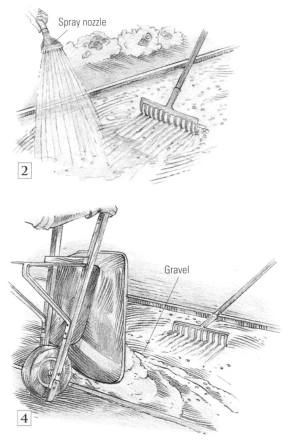

Gravel

Hand tamper

CUT STONE

A cut stone path or patio can be built easily, and sturdily, on a bed of sand. Design a simple or complex geometric pattern with the various sizes of squares and rectangles available, laying it out on paper before you shop. Edge your path or patio firmly, with lumber or an invisible concrete base. Loosen up the formal look, if you like, by planting between the stones.

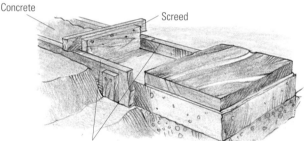

Concrete

Screed

Temporary forms

ON SAND OR MORTAR?

Cut stone laid on a bed of sand makes a durable and surprisingly sturdy path or patio, provided the edgings are strong, the stone is laid in a tight pattern, and the joints are kept tightly packed with sand. Occasional weeds in the joints can be kept down with a contact weed killer, and you can lay landscape fabric beneath the sand during the installation process to help suppress weeds (see page 85). Sand-bedding the stones provides a flexible surface that allows for easy repair should tree roots or frosts cause the underlying surface to buckle. Also, if a stone is damaged, it can be replaced easily if it has been laid in sand.

Placing the stones in mortar makes the path or patio surface more stable and permanent. Laying stone in wet mortar over a concrete slab provides the best protection against frost heaves and weed invasion. The dry-mortar method (stones are laid on sand, and dry mortar is brushed into the joints) provides some of this permanence with a lot less effort. See page 89 for instructions on wet and dry mortaring.

CHOOSING AN EDGING

If you are laying the stone in sand, make the edge of the path or patio secure by installing a 2-by-6 lumber edging (see page 84) flush with the cut stone surface. For invisible edgings, lay the stones around the edges of the path or patio on a concrete pad.

To form the pad, build temporary forms around the path or patio perimeter as if for a concrete footing. Make the forms the width of one stone and make the trench deep enough to allow for a 4-inch concrete bed (deeper where the ground freezes). Pour in concrete and, using a bladed screed, level it one stone thick below the top of the forms, as shown at left. Place the edging stones in the wet concrete, and set them with a rubber mallet. Remove the forms the next day. After the concrete has cured, lay the sand bed for the patio or path and the rest of the stone.

PATTERNS ON PAPER

Cut stone is usually available in squares and rectangles in several sizes, which allows you to make simple patterns with two sizes of stones or more complex patterns with many sizes. Rather than buying an assortment of shapes and sizes and making a jigsaw with them on the ground (don't step on them until they are bedded in sand or concrete because they may snap), work out the pattern on paper and then order the stones.

Note that the stones usually vary in size a little, so in your plan allow for an average ¼-inch gap between stones to accommodate the irregularities.

A SOLID BASE FOR CUT STONE

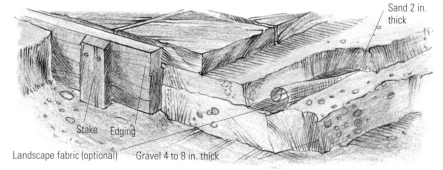

Sand 2 in. thick

Stake   Edging

Landscape fabric (optional)   Gravel 4 to 8 in. thick

LAYING CUT STONE IN SAND

To start, dig out the area to be paved to a depth of 4 inches—assuming 2 inches of sand and 2-inch-thick stones—and install the edgings. Dig deeper and lay 4 inches of compacted gravel below the sand if your soil drains poorly (lay 6 to 8 inches of compacted gravel if the ground freezes).

If you are laying a thin cut stone, like a ¾-inch-thick stone tile, figure on just ½ inch of sand or the stones may tilt when stepped on. Also, buy large pieces of stone, for example, 2 feet by 2 feet squares, which will be less likely to tilt than smaller pieces.

To help suppress weeds, lay landscape fabric on the ground (or between the sand and gravel if you are laying gravel).

Spend time screeding, or leveling, and tamping the moist sand so that it is thoroughly compacted. The firmer the base, the more stable the finished surface will be.

INSTALLING CUT STONE IN SAND

1 Spread a 2-inch-thick layer of dampened sand in the first section of the path or patio. Level the sand with a bladed screed, as shown. For a patio, use a temporary guide on which to rest one end of the screed. Tamp the sand after screeding; add more sand if needed, screed again, and tamp. Don't walk on the sand after you've done the final screeding.

2 Gently set the stones in position. Vary the size of the joints between stones to accommodate the variance in the stone cutting. Try not to slide the stones onto the sand—you'll displace sand from the bed and trap it between the stones. Lightly tap each stone into place with a rubber mallet. If a stone is twisted, realign it with a trowel blade. Check that it's level with a carpenter's level atop a piece of straight 2-by-4; if necessary, pry the stone out and add more sand or scoop some out.

3 When all the stones are in place, throw sand over them and sweep it into the joints. Wet the area with a light spray so the sand settles. Repeat the process several times until the sand is completely settled and about ¼ inch below the tops of the stone. Top up the joints with sand periodically to keep the stones tight.

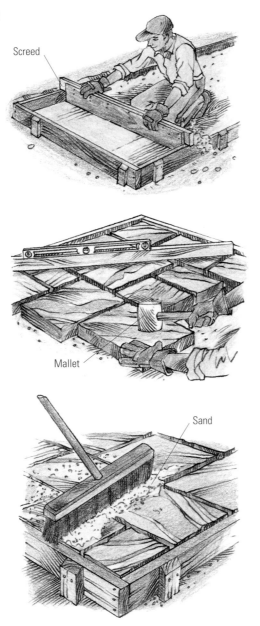

FORMAL LINES, INFORMAL PLANTINGS

The effect of nature reclaiming a few square inches of earth in a formal cut stone patio is so gladdening that it's worth building in as part of the plan. Finish screeding and tamping the sand bed, and then, as you're laying the stone, leave two or three spaces empty for plantings.

Tall plants are particularly effective in breaking up the formality of the stone. Because people will have to walk around them, choose places on the side of the patio or path, off the main traffic route. Consider planting the same species of plants that are growing in the garden proper to give the impression that they seeded naturally into the paving.

Bear in mind that the stability of the patio surface depends on the base being firm and stable. For each planting hole, excavate the sand and cut a cross in any landscape fabric. Work carefully as you incorporate soil into the planting holes. Avoid plants with aggressive or large root systems that might loosen the surrounding sand bed.

FLAGSTONE

Irregularly shaped flagstone is a versatile material. You can lay it in several different ways to make an informal paving surface or a more formal one. The most pleasing designs result from carefully fitting and trimming the stones.

ON SAND, MORTAR, OR SOIL?

Irregularly shaped flagstones can be laid in a bed of sand, with sand-packed joints or dry-mortared joints; in wet mortar over a concrete slab; or directly in stable soil. The last, obviously the easiest, is an option only if the stones are large and thick and not prone to breaking, and your soil is stable throughout the year. Consult the stone supplier before deciding on this option.

The sand-bed method with sand-packed joints (see page 87) provides a flexible surface that allows for easy repair should tree roots or frosts cause the underlying surface to buckle; plus, you can plant in the joints. The wet-mortar method provides the best protection against frost heaves and weed invasion. The dry-mortar method provides some of this permanence with a lot less effort.

WORKING WITH FLAGSTONE

Since most flagstones are irregularly shaped, you'll probably need to trim pieces before setting them. After you've marked out the perimeter of the path or patio, lay out the stones, shifting them around until you achieve a pleasing design that requires a minimum of cutting. If the stone is brittle or thin, don't step on it until it's bedded securely or it may snap.

You'll need gloves and safety glasses for even small trimming jobs. Chip off edges with a mason's hammer or a sharp brick set. To make a major cut, follow the steps shown below. Consider renting a portable saw with a masonry blade or, better still, a portable grinder fitted with a 4½-inch diamond wheel. It's often difficult to keep a stone from splitting or shattering beyond the cut line, so have some extra stone on hand.

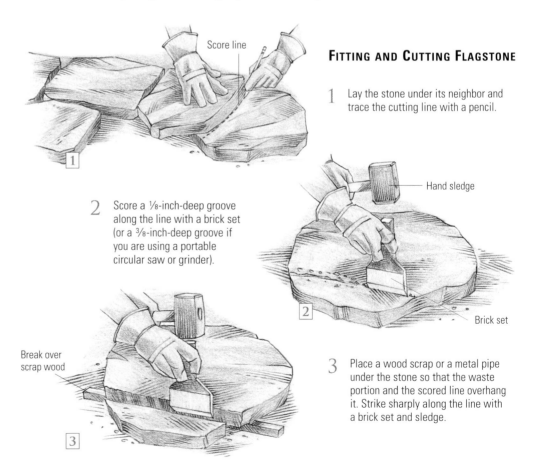

Score line

FITTING AND CUTTING FLAGSTONE

1 Lay the stone under its neighbor and trace the cutting line with a pencil.

2 Score a ⅛-inch-deep groove along the line with a brick set (or a ⅜-inch-deep groove if you are using a portable circular saw or grinder).

Hand sledge

Brick set

Break over scrap wood

3 Place a wood scrap or a metal pipe under the stone so that the waste portion and the scored line overhang it. Strike sharply along the line with a brick set and sledge.

LAYING FLAGSTONE WITH DRY-MORTARED JOINTS

To lay flagstone with dry-mortared joints, first make a sand bed and embed the stones in the sand, as described on page 87, steps 1 and 2. When all the stones are in place, mix dry cement and sand in a 1:3 ratio. Spread the dry mortar into the gaps between the stones, brushing it carefully off the stones. Then tamp it into the joints, using a piece of plywood. Add more mortar if needed. Carefully dust any remaining particles of mortar off the stones before wetting the surface.

Using an extremely fine spray, so as not to splash mortar out of the joints, wet down the path or patio surface. Don't allow pools to form, and try not to wash away any of the mortar. Over the next 2 to 3 hours, wet the paving periodically, keeping it damp. After a few hours, you can scrub the stones with burlap to help remove mortar stains. Should further cleaning be necessary, try a muriatic acid wash, but don't use this on limestone or marble, because the acid mars those types of stone.

LAYING FLAGSTONE IN WET MORTAR

For the wet-mortar method, you can either start with an existing concrete slab (it must be clean and in good condition, and at least 3 inches thick) or pour a new foundation. Ask your concrete dealer whether you need to use a bonding agent on the slab's surface. If the stones are porous, wet them a few hours before setting them to prevent them from absorbing too much water from the mortar. Sponge off any surface moisture before you place them in the mortar, to be certain you're getting a good bond.

First, arrange the stones on the concrete slab, cutting and trimming them so there's a minimum of space for mortar joints. Prepare a 1:3 cement-sand mortar mix, enough to cover 10 to 12 square feet. Add the water slowly. The mortar should be stiff enough to support the weight of the stones, but not so stiff that you can't work it (see page 91).

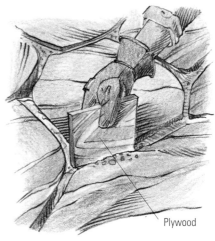

Plywood

The dry mortar mix is tamped into the joints to fill the gaps between the flagstone.

LAYING FLAGSTONE IN WET MORTAR

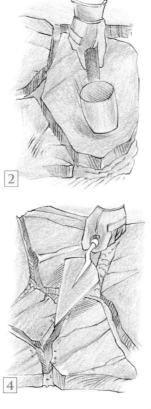

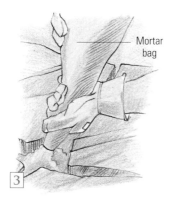

Mortar bag

1   Starting at one corner, remove a manageable section of stones and set them aside. Using a mason's trowel, spread at least enough mortar onto the slab to make a full mortar bed for one or two stones at a time. You'll need to vary the thickness of the mortar setting bed to make up for variations in stone thickness, but it should be at least 1 inch deep. Furrow the mortar with the trowel.

2   Set each stone firmly in place, bedding it by tapping it with a rubber mallet. To maintain an even surface, use a carpenter's level on a straight piece of 2-by-4. Clean the stones with a damp sponge as you work.

3   Let the mortar set for 24 hours, then grout the joints with mortar. Make the same mix you used for the setting bed, plus an optional ½ part fireclay to improve workability. If the stone is a staining type, use a mortar bag to squeeze the grout into the joints; otherwise use the trowel.

4   Smooth the joints with the trowel and clean up spills with a damp sponge. Keep the grout damp for the first day by sprinkling it with water or by covering it with plastic sheeting. Keep off the paved area for 3 days.

FIELDSTONES, COBBLES, PEBBLES, MOSAICS

There's nothing more rustic than a path or patio constructed of roughly flat stones—from field, riverbed, or beach—laid directly on the ground. However, if you place these stones in decorative patterns in concrete, you can create a look that's both playful and sophisticated. An existing concrete slab, provided it's in good condition, will do nicely as a base for a mortared mosaic of stones.

River stones

Set stones less than 6 inches in diameter in a mortar bed. Use a straight piece of 2-by-4 (right) to check for level.

LAYING LARGE FIELDSTONES AND COBBLES IN SOIL

Fieldstones and cobblestones 6 inches or more in diameter can be set directly in soil if your soil is stable. Arrange the fieldstones carefully so neighboring stones speak to each other—the concave side of one stone next to the convex side of another. For the most comfortable walking surface, lay them with their flattest sides up, and arrange the smallest cobbles in the center of the path, the larger ones on the edge.

Place the stones tightly together or leave gaps of up to 6 inches between stones. The larger the stones, the larger the gaps can be, which means more space for planting between the stones, if that's your plan, but small gaps make a more stable surface. Tap the stones into the soil with a rubber mallet, using a carpenter's level to check that the surface is more or less level. Pack the joints with gravel or, if you are going to plant in the joints, with a mixture of topsoil and sand. Water the paving surface to settle the gravel or soil between the stones, top up with more material if needed, and water again.

For a more permanent and weed-resistant path or patio, and a more stable surface on soils that buckle after frost, or that flood or crack, fieldstones and cobbles can be set in mortar on a concrete slab, as described below, or in a sand bed over gravel with a layer of landscape fabric to suppress weeds (see page 87).

Pebbles, cobbles, or fieldstones that are less than 6 inches in diameter should be set in mortar on a concrete slab or seeded into wet concrete.

SETTING SMALL STONES IN MORTAR

Small pebbles, cobbles, or fieldstones need to be set in mortar to make a stable, comfortable walking surface. Use an existing concrete slab for a base if it's clean and in good condition or build a new one. If you build a new one, leave the surface rough and let the concrete cure for at least 24 hours.

Prepare a 1:3 cement-sand mortar mixture and spread it over the slab to a depth of at least ½ inch (you'll need a deeper layer of mortar to accommodate thick stones or

stones that vary in thickness). Stones should be set in the mortar within 2 hours, so spread only as much mortar as you can fill within that time. Cut dry edges away from the previous mortar bed before spreading the new section. Keep porous stones in a pail of clean water, but sponge off the surface water before setting them in the mortar.

Push the stones in deep enough so the mortar gets a good hold on their edges—generally, just past the middle. Use a board to keep the stones level.

Let the mortar set for 2 to 3 hours; then spread another thin layer of mortar over the surface and into the voids. Hose and brush away any excess mortar before it sets.

SETTING SMALL STONES IN WET CONCRETE

A plain concrete patio or path can be jazzed up during construction by seeding pretty pebbles or varicolored aggregates into the freshly poured surface. Level the poured concrete about ½ inch lower than the form boards.

To seed tiny pebbles, sprinkle them evenly in a single layer over the slab. Using a block of wood, a float, or a darby, press the pebbles down until they lie just below the surface of the concrete. Using the same tool, refloat the concrete (smooth down high spots and fill hollows).

When the slab begins to harden, gently brush or broom the surface while wetting it down with a fine spray. Stop when the tops of the stones show. Any cement left on the stones can be removed later with a 10 percent muriatic acid solution.

For larger stones, push the stones into the concrete one by one, sinking slightly more than half the stone. When the concrete has hardened somewhat, expose the stones more by brushing the concrete while wetting down the surface with a fine spray.

MIXING MORTAR

Mortar recipes vary according to their intended use, but the ingredients are usually the same: cement, sand, possibly fireclay (do not use lime for stone projects, because it may leave stains), and water. Either make your own or buy more expensive ready-to-mix mortar. A typical mortar for stone paving consists of 1 part portland cement and 3 parts sand. To build a stone wall, you'll need a mix consisting of 1 part portland cement, ½ part fireclay, and 3 or 4 parts sand.

Small amounts of mortar can easily be mixed by hand, but mortar can be caustic, so be sure to wear gloves when you work with it. Carefully measure the sand, cement, and fireclay into a wheelbarrow or similar container. Use a hoe to thoroughly mix the dry ingredients and form them into a pile. Make a depression in the center of the dry mix and pour some water into it. Mix, then repeat the process.

When ready for use, mortar should have a smooth, uniform, granular consistency similar to oatmeal; it should also spread well and adhere to vertical surfaces (important when building a wall) but not "smear" the face of your work, which can happen when the mortar is too watery. Add water gradually until these conditions are met. Make only enough mortar to last a few hours; any more is likely to be wasted.

MOSAICS OF MIXED MATERIALS

All kinds of materials can be set into mortar to make a mosaic: glass, tile, china, mirror, beads, as well as the more common materials like pebbles and flagstones. The pattern is the key. Work it out on paper first, playing with all sorts of lines, geometric and free-form. Get ideas from books or wallpaper samples.

The most elegant mosaics employ a limited number of materials. The interest lies in the line and the slight natural variations in the stones' colors, which are more pronounced when wet. If the mosaic will be walked on, choose elements with a flattish surface, use a carpenter's level to keep the tops of the elements even, and mortar the gaps between them almost to the surface.

Lay the largest elements of the composition first. In the mosaic shown, note that large pieces of flagstone border the edges and smaller pieces serve as fill. The secret to laying small pebbles fairly quickly (either on their edges, as shown, or flat sides up) is to select pebbles that are very close in size.

BOULDERS

Installing boulders is vigorous, heavy work. Chances are the job is bigger than you think; you'll need fair-sized rock even for small projects, because the rock settles, often significantly. So plan for a team project, with help from friends, the rock yard, an equipment rental company, a contractor, maybe even a company that builds artificial rock.

MOVING BOULDERS BY HAND

Most people can't carry rocks that weigh more than 50 to 100 pounds. Somewhat larger rocks can be pushed and dragged with poles and boards as shown below. Use a piece of carpet instead of a board if the rocks have moss or lichen that might get scratched, and place carpet pads beneath ropes or chains to help prevent scuffs. Once a rock is in the hole you've prepared, a bar is useful if you need to turn it a few degrees.

You'll hear talk in the trade of one- and two-man rocks: rocks one or two men can move using 8-foot poles for leverage. A one-man rock weighs 300 pounds or less, a two-man rock as much as 900 pounds. Realistically, two men might find it strenuous work rolling a 500-pound boulder on level ground.

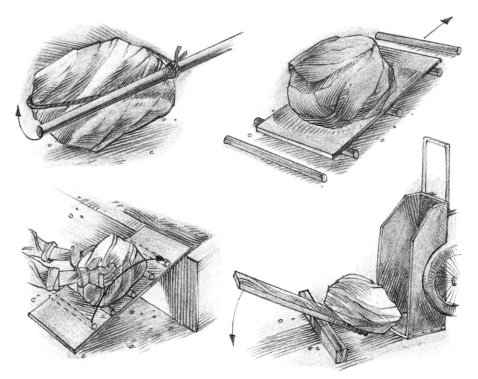

SAFETY FIRST

Wear leather gloves and sturdy boots, and stand to the side of the rock as you're moving it, so that if it rolls, it doesn't roll into you. To lift a small rock without injuring yourself, take these precautions: bend your knees, keep your back straight, hold the load firmly, and then straighten your knees, elbows close to your sides. Never try to lift a rock too heavy for you; instead, roll it up a plank set on an incline and lever it into place.

Transport rocks in a cart rather than a single-wheel wheelbarrow, because the weight can easily shift and tip a barrow over. If you are installing several boulders on a sloping site, start work at the foot of the slope and embed each rock securely, back and down into the slope, before moving uphill.

WORKING WITH PROFESSIONALS

Install a 2-ton rock and decide it doesn't look natural, and you're stuck. So think about working with a landscape architect, designer, or contractor who has done excellent installations of rock. If you live on a sloping lot, you may need to consult a landscape architect to ascertain whether the slope can hold the rocks securely.

Most rock yards will deliver rock in a dump truck, leaving it for you to put in place. For bigger rocks, find a yard that has a boom-equipped truck that can not only deliver the load but also dig holes and use the boom to set each rock in place. Alternatively, consider renting a loader with a back hoe and a bucket attachment for a day (see Contractors' Equipment and Supplies in the Yellow Pages), or make it a clean professional job by hiring a crane and watching the boulder spin into place in no time.

Take snapshots of the rocks when you pick them out at the yard, and decide exactly where and how you want each rock placed before the delivery truck arrives or you rent equipment. Make dummy rocks with garbage bags filled with newspaper to help you decide on the final placement. Plan the access route to each of your rock sites and think about whether there's adequate space to maneuver heavy equipment.

ARTIFICIAL ROCK

In some gardens, site conditions or access problems make it impossible to install natural rock. If that's the case in your yard, perhaps consider an artificial product that has been shaped, textured, and colored to resemble natural stone.

Artificial rock is manufactured in different ways. One method starts with a boulder-shaped frame of reinforcing bar. Wire mesh or metal lath is secured to the frame; then several layers of concrete are applied. To re-create the cracks and fissures of natural rock, the still wet concrete may be carved with tools or embossed with crinkled aluminum foil, clear plastic wrap, or custom latex molds cast from rock formations. To imitate the pastiche of colors in natural rock, the flecks of lichen, and the specks of soil, manufacturers color the concrete by brushing, spraying, or splattering on diluted acrylic stains.

Artificial rock can be used for steps, waterfalls, and ponds, and also to mask retaining walls. Because of labor and materials, the cost of artificial rock is usually slightly higher than that of real stone or boulders.

PLACING BOULDERS NATURALLY

To look like part of the natural bedrock, rocks need to be settled into the earth. The general rule is to bury the bottom one third of the rock; alternatively, sink the rock into the ground to just beyond its widest point. Avoid placing a rock so that it looks undercut or top heavy; unless you do this artfully, the rock will merely seem unstable. For the same reason, don't put a large rock on top of a small one. Allow for the settling of large rocks, because the amount can be significant.

A natural-looking composition of many rocks takes careful planning. Use just one type of stone, in various sizes, with at least one or two 500-pound boulders as anchors, and think architecturally—try to establish related planes and lines. Natural outcroppings of stratified sedimentary rock offer a good model. To mimic those lines, lay the stones in a series of bands parallel to one another (see below left). Place each stone so that its longest side lies along the direction of the band. The top of each stone should be on the same plane, either horizontal or tilted slightly upward, all at the same angle (see below right). The composition looks restful when the stones are carefully related, and all conflicting lines and planes are avoided.

Some fieldstones, especially those of volcanic origin, can be hard to compose into natural-looking groups. Start by finding the flattest side and placing that side up. Keep the top of each stone on the same plane as every other stone in the garden.

Rocks look better with time. Scars from transport and handling disappear, and lichen grows if you live where the air is relatively unpolluted. After the lichen has formed a wash over the rock and roughed up its surface, moss may move in if it's native to rocks in your part of the country.

PLACING BOULDERS NATURALLY

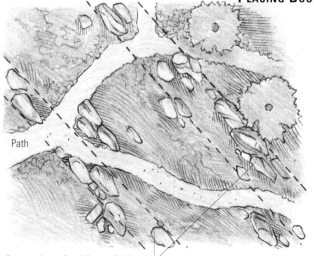

Outcroppings of rock in parallel bands

Path

The top of each stone tilts at the same angle

STEPS

Steps emphasize a change in the lay of the land. It's up to you how dramatically to mark it—with a straight-up-and-down formal staircase made of cut stone (a complex construction project not described here) or with a series of gravel steps or stepping-stones that weave across the slope and take the bite, and some of the drama, out of the climb. Draw out various ways of fitting steps into the slope gracefully; then settle on the plan that's most suitable for the volume of traffic and your garden style.

GRACIOUS DIMENSIONS

Well-designed steps have good proportions: the flat part of the step, called the tread, is nicely in proportion to the vertical element, the riser. A model step, based on an average length of stride, has a 6-inch-high riser and a generous 15-inch-deep tread.

The tread can be as little as 11 inches deep, but never less if you want the steps to feel comfortable, and the riser from 5 to 8 inches high, but choose dimensions that relate to one another. The formula for good proportions is as follows: the depth of the tread plus twice the riser height should equal 25 to 27 inches, as shown in the chart. For safety's sake, make all the risers and treads in any one flight of steps uniform in size.

IDEAL TREAD-RISER RELATIONSHIP

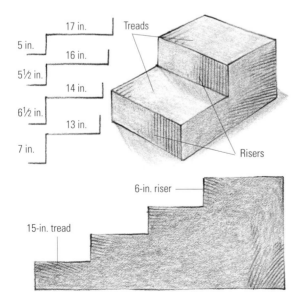

5 in. — 17 in. — Treads
5½ in. — 16 in.
6½ in. — 14 in.
7 in. — 13 in. — Risers

6-in. riser
15-in. tread

FITTING STEPS TO THE SLOPE

Using the drawing as a guide, calculate the distance from A to B; this is the change in level, or rise, of the slope. The distance from A to C is called the run. If the rise is less than 10 percent, that is, less than 1 foot in every 10 feet of run, and the material you'll be using for the path isn't slippery, the slope is gentle enough not to require steps (though you might still install one or two as a pleasing design detail).

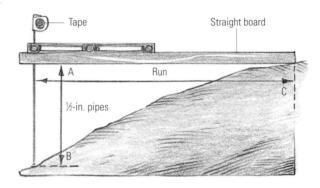

Tape | Straight board
A | Run
½-in. pipes | C
B

To determine the number of steps you'll need, divide the desired riser height into the total rise of the slope (in inches). If the answer ends in a fraction (and it probably will), drop the fraction and divide the whole number into the vertical distance; the resulting figure will give you the exact measurement for each of your risers.

Check the chart to see whether the corresponding minimum tread will fit into the slope's total run. Rarely will the steps fit exactly into a slope as it is. Plan to cut and fill the slope, as shown on page 98, to accommodate the steps.

If your slope is too steep even for 8-inch risers, remember that steps need not run straight up and down. Consider taking the steps through curves and switchbacks up the slope, and breaking up any single flight of steps more than 5 feet high with one or more landings. This will make the walking distance longer but the climb much less daunting.

Plan on a width of 2 feet for utility steps. For other steps, 4 feet is a good minimum width, 5 feet if you want two people to be able to walk along together.

TIMBERS OR TIES WITH GRAVEL TREADS

Gravel with railroad ties or 6-by-6 pressure-treated timbers make a simple, rugged set of steps. Installation is relatively easy, but if you are using railroad ties you may need a helper because they are quite heavy.

Excavate the site to the shape of the steps, tamping the soil in the tread area very firmly. Lay the ties or timbers on the soil, then drill a hole near each end of the ties or timbers. With a

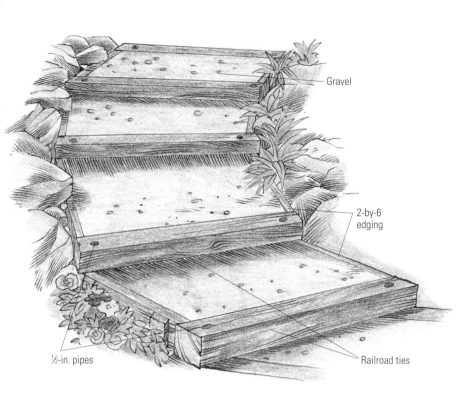

Gravel

2-by-6 edging

½-in. pipes

Railroad ties

A SINGLE STEP

One stone step accents very simply the slope on a path. But it must be extra large and clearly visible or people will not notice it and may trip. Once you've chosen the stone, ask the supplier to cut it in two, for easier transportation. Then put the pieces back together alongside one another in the excavated path, and fill the crack with gravel. Try to choose a stone that came from the same quarry as the gravel so that they have the same character.

sledge, drive either ½-inch galvanized steel pipes or ¾-inch reinforcing bars through the holes into the ground.

Or, for extra support, pour small concrete footings and set anchor bolts in the slightly stiffened concrete. When the concrete has set (after about 2 days), secure the ties to the footings with the bolts.

Once the tie or timber risers are in place, excavate the tread spaces behind them. Install 2-by-6 lumber edgings (see page 84). Lay a 1-inch bed of sand, compact it, and fill the spaces with gravel, tamping it firmly (see page 85).

A STEPPING-STONE STAIRCASE

A stepping-stone staircase is another relatively easy and inexpensive way to take a path up a slope. It works particularly well in an informal area of the garden and where foot traffic isn't high. Choose extra large, thick stones, at least 20 inches deep, 2 feet wide, and 6 to 8 inches thick.

Starting at the downhill end of the slope, excavate a hole for the first stone. Make it 6 to 8 inches deep, depending on the thickness of your stone. Spread 2 inches of sand in the bottom of the hole, wet the sand, and tamp it. Lay the stone on the sand and twist it into the sand until it is level and firmly embedded. The surface of the stone should sit about 2 inches above grade, so that soil doesn't wash onto it.

When the first stone is securely embedded, position the next stone. In gentle sections of the path, space the stones as you would for a stepping-stone path (see pages 82–83). Where the slope is steep, overlap the stones a few inches, for stability, and spread a 1-inch layer of mortar (optional) at the back of the lower step, to bond them where they touch.

If your soil is unstable or drains poorly, install 4 to 6 inches of tamped gravel beneath the sand.

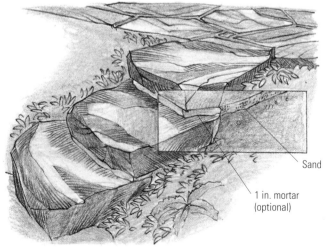

Sand

1 in. mortar (optional)

FREESTANDING WALLS

A dry-stone wall can be a relatively simple project—no concrete footings, no mortar—but whether the wall is dry laid or mortared, it needs to be constructed artfully, with a natural-looking arrangement of stones.

ATTRACTIVE FITTING

The key to building an attractive stone wall is careful fitting. Properly placed, the stones make a harmonious and pleasing pattern, and the finished wall looks like a unit rather than a random pile of rocks.

Neatly trimmed ashlar stone is relatively easy to lay in pleasing regular courses. Fitting untrimmed or roughly trimmed rubble, which comes in many shapes and sizes, takes more time. Unless the stones have been at least roughly squared, it won't be possible to lay them in horizontal courses; you'll need to build an agreeable arrangement of irregular shapes. For ease of fitting, choose flat stones rather than round ones. For an interesting pattern, choose a range of sizes—from stones that are at least 6 inches long or high to stones 6 times that size. Place the very largest stones at the base of the wall, and generally orient every stone as it would lie naturally on the ground—not on end or in an obviously unnatural position.

BUILDING CODES

Many municipalities require a building permit for any wall more than 3 feet high, so be sure to check before you start. There may also be regulations that specify how close to your property line you can build, or what kind of foundation you'll need.

STRONG BONDING

To make a wall strong, always follow the stonemason's basic rule: "One stone over two, two over one." That way, every vertical joint is staggered; there's overlap with the stone above and the one below.

Freestanding walls are usually laid up in two wythes (vertical stacks) with rubble fill between them. Bond stones, equivalent to headers in brickwork, run across the width of the wall, tying it together. Use as many bond stones as possible—at least 1 for every 10 square feet of wall surface.

Most walls should slope inward on both sides. This tilting of the faces is called "batter" and helps secure the wall, since the faces lean on each other. The amount of batter depends on the size and purpose of the wall, the shape of stones used, and whether the wall is mortared. A good rule of thumb is to plan 1 to 2 inches of batter for each 2 feet of rise—more if stones are very round and less if they are well-trimmed ashlar. Mortared walls can get by with less batter, or no batter if the wall is low.

To check the tilt on a wall, make a batter gauge by taping together a 2-by-4 board, a scrap block, and a carpenter's level. When using the gauge, keep the outer edge plumb with the level.

BUILDING A DRY-STONE WALL

A dry-stone wall is constructed directly on the ground and without mortar. It depends upon the weight and friction of one stone on another for its stability. If you are a beginner, give the wall a broad base—for a wall 3 feet high, make the base at least 2 feet wide and considerably wider if the stone is very round. Usually, only skilled stonemasons can construct a narrow dry-stone wall with faces that are almost vertical.

Place your stones near the site for convenience while you're building the wall and sort out the stones before you begin. Use the largest stones for the foundation course, and set aside the longer ones for bond stones and the broad, flat stones for capping the top of the wall.

USING A BATTER GAUGE

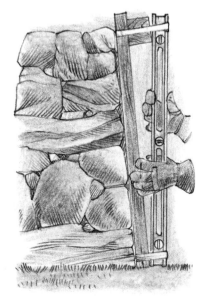

BUILDING A MORTARED STONE WALL

Building a wall with mortar allows you to use almost any kind of stone, including very round stones. A mortared wall up to 3 feet high also needs little or no batter. However, a mortared wall more than 12 inches high needs a large concrete footing—extending below the frost line (in frost-free areas, a 12-inch-deep footing is sufficient for a 3-foot wall) and about half again as wide as the wall. For a very low wall, you can lay the base of the wall on tamped soil or in a leveled trench.

Unless you are an experienced do-it-yourselfer, have a contractor make the wooden forms for the footing and pour the concrete. Once the footing is installed, building a mortared wall is similar to building a dry-stone wall.

BUILDING A DRY-STONE WALL

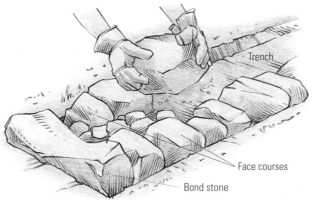

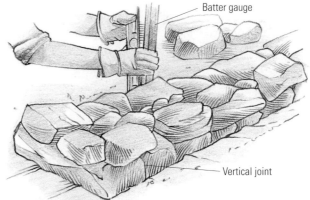

1 Lay the foundation stones in a trench about 6 inches deep. First, place a bond stone at each end; then start the two face courses at both edges of the trench. Choose whole, well-shaped stones for the face courses. Fill in the space between the face courses with tightly packed rubble (broken pieces of stone).

2 Lay stones atop the first course, being sure to stagger vertical joints. Select stones that will fit together solidly. Tilt the stones of each face inward toward one another. Use the batter gauge on the faces and ends of the wall to check the tilt. Place bond stones every 5 to 10 square feet to tie the faces of the wall together. Again, pack the center with rubble and small stones.

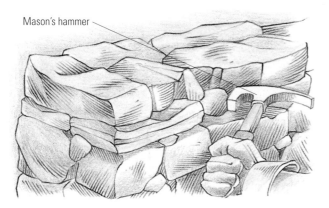

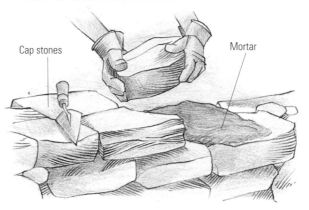

3 Continue to add courses, staggering vertical joints and maintaining the inward slope, so that gravity and the friction of the stones set one upon another will help hold the wall together. Gently tap small stones into any gaps with a mason's hammer, but don't overdo it: driving them in too tight might dislodge stones you've already set.

4 Finish the top with as many flat, broad stones as possible. If you live in an area that experiences frost, mortar the cap as shown. This will allow water to drain off the wall and help prevent ice from forming between the stones and pushing them apart. Don't rake or make indents in these joints; level them flush with a piece of scrap wood to prevent water from collecting.

BUILDING A MORTARED WALL

Spread a 1-inch-thick mortar bed at one end of the footing and set the first bond stone, making sure it is well bedded. Then start the two face courses at both edges of the footing, spreading a mortar bed as you work. Pack joints between stones with mortar, and fill the space between the front and back faces solidly with rubble and mortar. For each subsequent course, build a mortar bed over the previous course of stones; then set the new row of stones in place, placing a bond stone every 5 to 10 square feet and offsetting vertical joints. Dry-fit the stones before spreading the mortar bed and fill large gaps with small stones. As you work, check the alignment of the stones and the plumb or batter on the wall faces. After you've laid a section, use a piece of wood to rake out the joints to a depth of ½ to ¾ inches. Clean up spilled mortar from the face of the stone with a wet sponge as you work.

RETAINING WALLS

A retaining wall holds back soil, whether it's soil for a raised planting bed or an entire hillside. Team up with experts to build a tall retaining wall; let them do the building department–approved structural work with concrete block, and then, if you like, you can veneer stone to the surface. Or keep the wall low and simple and be conscientious about building only on undisturbed, stable ground and laying a drainpipe.

BUILDING CODES

Simple stone retaining walls, less than 3 feet high and on a gentle slope with stable soil, can be built by a do-it-yourselfer, but it's still a good idea to consult your local building department. Most communities require a building permit for any retaining wall and even may require a soil analysis in an area suspected of being unstable.

GRADING AND DRAINING THE SLOPE

If space permits, the safest way to build a retaining wall is to locate it at the bottom of a gentle slope and fill in behind it with soil. Or a hill can be held with a series of low walls that form terraces, or with a single high wall. All three methods are shown below. Notice that in each case the retaining wall rests on cut or undisturbed ground, never on fill. If extensive grading is required, hire a professional.

A solid retaining wall acts like a dam, restricting the flow of water above and below ground, so you must make some provision for drainage or risk bursting the wall. Usually, you'll need a gravel backfill behind the wall to collect the subsurface water and either weep holes in the base of the wall to drain it or a drainpipe in the gravel that channels the water into a storm sewer or other disposal area.

A SIMPLE MODULAR RETAINING WALL

A low, fairly stable slope can be retained by a dry-stone or mortared stone wall (see pages 96–97) or one of the several simple modular masonry systems developed for the do-it-yourselfer. The modular systems consist of interlocking concrete blocks with rough finishes like split rock; a planter version is available, with a hollow center for soil and plants. A modular block wall needs a simple gravel footing and gravel backfill with a drainpipe—no concrete work or mortar. Because the blocks interlock in such a way that they create a uniform setback into the slope, you don't need to batter the wall.

For a modular system, shown at the top of the next page, dig a trench 2 feet wide and 6 inches deeper than the thickness of the block. String mason's twine to mark the front edge of the wall. Pour 6 inches of gravel into the trench and compact it firmly with a hand tamper. Check that the base is level.

Lay the foundation row of blocks on the gravel footing. If the blocks have a rear lip, install this first row upside down and backward, so that the block surface that rests on the gravel is flat and the lip is facing up at the front of the wall. Check that the blocks are level and aligned with the twine.

Lay perforated drainpipe, perforated side down, on the gravel behind the wall. Pack gravel under the pipe as needed to ensure the open end slopes downhill toward the water disposal area.

Lay the second row of blocks, staggering the joints in a running bond pattern. Backfill the space behind the wall with gravel, and tamp the gravel firmly with a hand tamper. Place the next and subsequent rows of blocks in the same manner, backfilling and compacting the gravel after laying each row.

Lay landscape fabric over the gravel backfill before you replace the topsoil and plant behind the wall. The fabric will help prevent soil from clogging the gravel backfill.

GRADING THE SLOPE

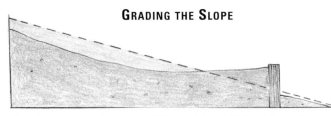

Slope is cut away and excess earth is moved downhill. Retaining wall now holds back long, level terrace.

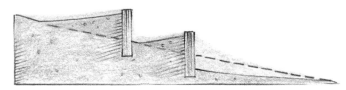

Total wall height is divided between two terraces, resulting in a series of level beds.

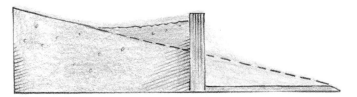

Earth is cut away and moved behind tall retaining wall. Result is level ground below and a high level slope behind.

A MODULAR RETAINING WALL

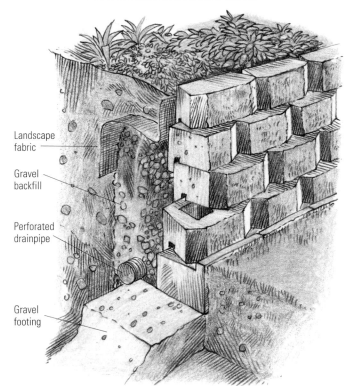

Landscape fabric

Gravel backfill

Perforated drainpipe

Gravel footing

Interlocking blocks make a simple retaining wall.

A STONE-VENEERED WALL

Metal wall tie

1 in. mortar

Veneer stones

Concrete blocks

A reinforced concrete block wall can be veneered with stone.

A STONE-VENEERED CONCRETE BLOCK WALL

Walls built of concrete blocks are good for holding steep or unstable hillsides, and they can be veneered with natural stone to look like a solid stone wall. Unless you're an experienced do-it-yourselfer, have a qualified contractor build the block wall, reinforced as necessary to meet the building department's specifications, and do the veneering yourself.

Make sure that noncorrosive metal wall ties, spaced 2 to 3 feet apart, are inserted in the mortar joints in every other row of blocks. You'll bend them into the joints between your stones to anchor the stones to the wall.

If you are mortaring stone onto an existing concrete block wall, excavate to the concrete footing, clean the surface of the wall and footing, and let it dry before you start. Put metal wall ties in place as described above, nailing them into the blocks, not the joints.

Be sure to buy veneer stone, which is cut to a uniform thickness, and face the roughest side outward. Refer to the information on attractive fitting on page 96.

Make a dryish mortar mix, about the consistency of oatmeal, from 1 part portland cement, ½ part fireclay, and 3 or 4 parts sand. A dry mortar will dry more quickly, and it won't run out of the joints so easily.

Place 1 inch of mortar on the wall footing and lay the first stone 1 inch from the wall. Check the mortar; it should be dry enough to hold the stone. Completely fill the space between the stone and the wall with mortar . Then, continue to lay the first course of stones along the length of the wall as you would for a freestanding wall (see page 97).

Lay the second course of stones, following the stonemason's rule of "one stone over two, two over one." Mortar each stone to the stones beneath it and to the wall, filling the spaces completely. Fit the stones so that you can bend the wall ties into the joints between the courses. Put a little mortar on the top of the lower stone, bend the tie onto the mortar, add another layer of mortar over it, and set the stone on top.

Place large, flat stones on the top of the wall to form a cap, with the edges overhanging the side of the wall by 1 inch. Mortar the stones together and to the top of the wall.

BOWLS, BIRDBATHS, AND FOUNTAINS

Stone water bowls and birdbaths make simple decorative details in the garden. Place them so that the water shines with sunlight, and keep them filled to the brim. Pebble and boulder fountains are also prettiest in sunlight, because it makes the water spray sparkle as it flies through the air; but build one somewhere out of the wind, so that the water trickles back reliably to the reservoir.

SITING A WATER BOWL

Experiment to find the best place for a water bowl. Place it in an open area, and the water will sparkle with reflections of the sky. Under a tree, it'll catch the dark reflections of the undersides of the leaves. Whether the water will reflect what you want it to depends on the position of the sun in relation to the object and your eye. Set it up somewhere and check the reflections as you approach it along the path or look down on it from the deck. If the bowl seems too small once it's in position, raise it on bricks or concrete pavers, or set it on top of a pedestal or small column.

Using a carpenter's level, check that the rim of the bowl is perfectly even before filling it with water. Once it's full, it'll be too heavy and awkward to move, and even a slight tilt will be evident in the water line. Moisten the soil under the bowl, if necessary, and screw the bowl into the soft soil.

SITING A BIRDBATH

To be popular with the birds, a birdbath must be placed so that it looks safe from predators. Elevate it out of the reach of cats, and perhaps place it near a tree or shrub; birds will alight in the branches and then when they've judged that the sights are clear, they'll hop onto the rim of the birdbath.

Check that the rim of the birdbath is perfectly level. Because birds love fresh water, refill the bowl frequently. If there's an irrigation line nearby, consider clipping an emitter to the back of the bowl.

THE MECHANICS OF MOVING WATER

Fountains generally require a pump, which is hidden in the bottom of the pond or in a water reservoir that's out of sight. An electrical cable extends from the submerged pump to a GFI outlet, a safe, waterproof, outdoor electricity socket. Have an electrician install a GFI outlet if necessary, and buy a pump with a cable that is long enough to reach from the bottom of the pond or the water reservoir to the outlet. Where the cable crosses the garden, keep it safe from the sharp blade of a spade, or a child playing with a sharp object, by running it through a 1-inch PVC pipe and burying the pipe in the ground.

Fountains are of two main types: jets of water that spray upward in different shapes from a fountainhead nozzle screwed onto the pump; and sheets of water that splash from the top of a statue or a chute, the water coming from plastic tubing that's attached to an outlet on the pump and taken to the top of the fountain. Consult a pump supplier about a suitable pump for your fountain; the larger the water flow and the greater the head (the vertical distance from the surface of the pond or reservoir to the top of the jet or chute), the bigger the pump you'll need.

A few simple solar-powered fountains are available, comprised of a disk that contains solar panels and a small pump. The disk floats on the water surface, and when heat activates the panels, the pump sends a spray of water into the air.

MAKING A PEBBLE FOUNTAIN

A pebble fountain is relatively easy to make. In a windy location, choose a low, gushing fountainhead rather than a thin, tall jet so the water doesn't fly away in the wind.

PEBBLE FOUNTAIN

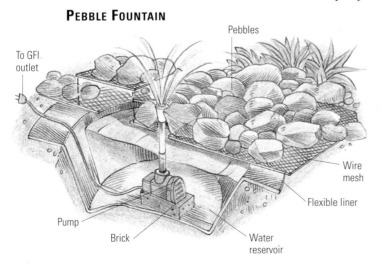

To GFI. outlet
Pebbles
Pump
Brick
Water reservoir
Wire mesh
Flexible liner

Make the reservoir using a black liner, a preformed pond shell, or any kind of large watertight container that is at least 15 inches deep. The reservoir can be just 18 inches wide or as much as 3 feet wide or even wider. Consider the spray pattern from the fountainhead and how windy the site is, and know that if you make the reservoir small, you'll need to remember to fill it frequently during hot or windy weather to ensure that the water level never drops below the pump.

Place the pump in the reservoir on top of a clean brick so the silt that collects on the reservoir bottom doesn't enter the pump. Fit a rigid extension pipe to the pump outlet and screw the fountainhead onto the top of the pipe. The fountainhead should just clear the top of the reservoir. Trim the extension pipe if necessary or raise the pump to reach the correct height. Take the electrical cable out over the edge of the reservoir in the direction of the GFI outlet.

Place a piece of strong wire mesh over the reservoir, making sure it overlaps the water edge by at least 6 inches. Cut a square out of the mesh, big enough to put your hand through comfortably, so that you can reach the pump to adjust the water flow or clear the filter screen. Place a large square of mesh over the square you've cut out; it should be large enough not to sag once it's covered with pebbles.

Fill the reservoir with water. Place a few large pebbles on the edges of the wire mesh to secure it, then cover the rest of the mesh with pebbles. Mark the access to the pump with a few highly colored or glass pebbles. Turn on the electricity and check the jet spray; adjust the water flow on the pump if necessary to ensure that the spray stays within the circle of stones and drips back into the reservoir.

INSTALLING A BOULDER FOUNTAIN

Some suppliers of stone boulders sell stones already drilled for a fountain pipe or will drill a boulder of your choice. The installation is similar to making a pebble fountain.

Make the reservoir. Then put a layer of liner protection fabric on the bottom and build two columns of concrete block or flat stones to support the boulder. Place the pump on a brick between the columns, screw an extension pipe onto the pump outlet, and install wire mesh over the reservoir. Lower the boulder into position, making sure it is well supported by the columns. Place pebbles around the boulder.

BOULDER FOUNTAIN

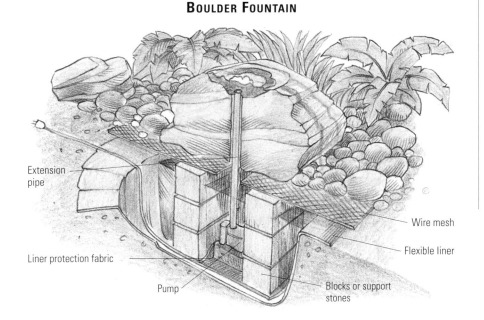

Extension pipe

Liner protection fabric

Pump

Wire mesh

Flexible liner

Blocks or support stones

BAMBOO AND STONE FOUNTAIN

The water seems to spill naturally off the steep bank through a bamboo pipe someone has placed there. There's a pump, of course, in the pond below the mossy stone bowl, with an electrical cable that plugs into a GFI outlet behind a stone, and plastic tubing that runs from the pump up through the wall, or underneath the ferns on the wall, into the bamboo spill pipe.

Bamboo is not naturally completely hollow; it has a layer of corky membrane at each node, which you will have to drill through to insert the plastic tubing (unless you buy bamboo already prepared for use in a fountain). To get the tubing through the bamboo to within an inch of the spill point, drop one end of a chain through the bamboo. Pry open the last link in the chain and pierce the tubing with it, so they are firmly attached. Pull on the end of the chain, threading the tubing through the bamboo.

Pond Edgings and Beaches

In a garden with stone paths or other stone features, stone makes a natural edging for a pond. Lay a flagstone or cut stone path to the water's edge using large paving pieces and securing the edge, if necessary, so the stones don't slide in. Or use any kind of stone—boulders, fieldstones, cobbles, pebbles, gravel—to cover up the place where the liner or pond shell meets land.

Paving the Pond Edge

Before you begin to edge a pond with paving stone, such as flagstone or cut stone, consider whether people will be walking to the water's edge. If the answer is yes, for safety's sake choose extralarge stone (say, 3 feet by 3 feet), so that the weight is distributed away from the pond edge. If your soil is unstable, consider having a 4-inch-thick reinforced concrete footing poured around the pond, or the section of the pond where there will be access, to firmly support the stones.

Fieldstones and pebbles can be set at the pond edge using the method described here for paving stone. But avoid ringing the pond with an unnatural "necklace" of small bumpy stones.

After installing the pond, fill it with water and let the pond settle for a week, if possible, before laying the stone edge. Make the mortar mix for the base with 1 part cement and 3 parts sand. If you buy a premixed mortar, make sure it contains no lime, because lime fouls pond water.

To edge a pond built with a preformed shell, take precautions to avoid buckling the rim. Do not lay the stones directly on the rim, not even to dry-fit them. Spread a 3-inch-thick base of mortar that sits slightly higher than the rim, as shown at left, so that the embedded stones are supported by the mortar and sit above the rim.

To edge a pond built with a flexible liner, follow the steps illustrated at right.

Edging stone

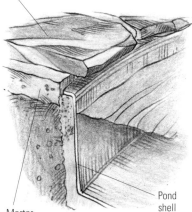
Mortar
Pond shell

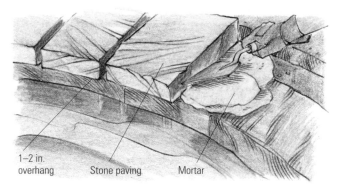
1–2 in. overhang   Stone paving   Mortar

1 With the pool filled, trim the liner so it extends 4 or 5 inches over the edging shelf. Lay a dry run of stones, the front edge of each stone overhanging the pond rim by 1 to 2 inches, and do any necessary cutting of the stones (see page 88) to make the edging fit perfectly. Remove the stones, spread a thin layer of mortar on the shelf, and set the stones in place.

2 Bed each stone firmly into position by tapping it with a rubber mallet. Use a straightedge (a long piece of straight 2-by-4) and a carpenter's level to check that the edging is even. Clean mortar splashes from the stones with a sponge and water as you work.

3 Let the spread mortar set for 24 hours. Then make a fresh mortar mix, adding ½ part fireclay to make it more workable, and pack mortar between the stones. Smooth the joints with a pointing trowel. (Do not use muriatic acid solution to clean spilled mortar if your edging is made of limestone or marble, because it will mar those types of stone.) Keep off the edging for 3 days to let the mortar harden.

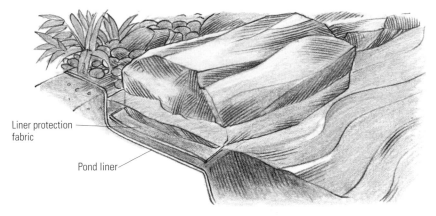

PLACING A BOULDER IN A POND

Liner protection
fabric

Pond liner

PLACING BOULDERS

The edge of a steep-sided pond made with a liner or preformed shell is not always sufficiently sturdy to take the weight of a boulder. Preformed shells may warp, or the edge may cave and the soil slide under the liner. Constructing the pond with concrete or supporting the edge with concrete block or a concrete collar will provide a very sturdy edge. The simpler option is not to place the boulders on the rim, but to put them either outside of the pond edging or inside the pond itself.

Choose low, almost flat, or dome-shaped boulders for places outside of the pond. These shapes are naturally widest at the base so they will look stable and solid when settled only an inch or two into the soil. To prevent the pond edge from crumbling, disturb the soil as little as possible as you position the boulders.

Boulders can sit on the pond bottom, or on a marginal shelf if it's sufficiently stable. Place liner protection fabric between each boulder and the pond liner or shell, and be extremely careful not to rip the side of the pond while installing the boulders. Settle them into a bed of rounded gravel if they have sharp edges or need stabilizing.

CREATING A BEACH

Beaches are suitable for ponds with gradually sloping sides or a wide shallow shelf or bog area around the edge. Choose rounded water-washed stones, pebbles, and gravels for a natural look. If any of the materials have sharp edges, lay liner protection fabric beneath them. Wash the stones before placing them in the pond.

Moisture-loving plants and bog plants can be grown in a trough of soil above the waterline on a gently sloping pond edge. A ridge of earth, shown below right, prevents pebbles on a wide shelf from slipping into the bottom of the pond.

INFORMAL PATH AND POND EDGING

One of the ways to avoid an unnatural-looking ring of stone around a pond is to spread the same stone back into the garden, and put it to use as stepping-stones or decorative screes below boulders. Another way is to vary the pond edging, placing flat stones very securely on one side so there's access to the water, and planting the far edge thickly or placing boulders there. Note the gray-blue gravel stream winding its way to the flagstone shore. It doesn't actually slope downhill, or water might run off it into the pond.

Flexible liner

Planting area in trough
on gentle slope

Ridge

Wide shelf

WATERFALLS, STREAMS, AND DRY CREEKBEDS

Building a natural-looking wet stream or waterfall requires two skills: making a waterproof channel, so the water doesn't escape, and being creative at mimicking how water flows in nature. The work is reduced by half if you choose a dry stream or waterfall, and if you place the stones well, you'll almost be able to hear the water chuckle and splash.

BUILDING A SIMPLE WATERFALL

The simplest waterfall is a single step fall, with the water flowing from an upper pond over a spill stone into a lower pond. Being simple and small, it's far more credible, visually, for a garden than a towering cascade, and the sound is more soothing. Use the soil you excavate for the ponds to make a gentle slope if you don't have a natural slope in your garden. Avoid an unnatural-looking mound, and compact the soil thoroughly before installing the waterfall.

The pump for the falls sits in the lower pond; plastic tubing attached to the pump outlet and taken over the edge of the pond inconspicuously between rocks delivers water to the top of the falls (see page 100).

Excavate the two ponds; the lower one should be significantly larger than the upper one (if you like, make the upper pond a stream). Make a firm shelf in the lower pond for the waterfall stones. As you lay the liner protection fabric and the pond liner, leave plenty of both in the area of the waterfall, so that you can bring them up behind the spill stone and surrounding rocks, as shown.

Place another piece of liner protection fabric on the shelf, over the liner. Then position the waterfall backing stone and the spill stone on the ledge, settling the backing stone into a bed of gravel if it has sharp edges. The stones must be secure: lift the liner and fabric and reinforce the ledge with small stones set into the soil if necessary, or, if the waterfall stones are very heavy, with concrete block or a 4-inch pad of concrete.

Stack taller rocks on each side of the waterfall stones, to channel the water and give a sense that water scored a gorge between them. Place liner protection fabric beneath each rock and ensure it is stable before positioning the next rock.

Line the upper pond. Secure the liner and liner protection fabric behind the waterfall with one or two rocks. Take the liner from the upper pond over the liner from the lower pond, as shown.

Fill the ponds, plug in the pump, and run the waterfall to check the rock placement and water flow. The spill stone may need adjusting so that the water spills off the edge of it in a sheet. Tilting it forward will help send the water over the edge in a proper spill. If the water persists in trickling down the face of the spill stone, consider mortaring an acrylic lip to the stone. To make a bigger splash at the base of the falls, place a rock there to break up the water. While you have the water running, check for leaks, especially where the liner pieces overlap.

Once the rocks seem well placed and the sound of the water is pleasant, drain the ponds, mortar gaps between the rocks by the falls so that water flows over the stones not beneath them, apply a waterproof sealer to the mortar, and finish the pond edgings (see pages 102–103).

MAKING A DRY CREEKBED

A realistic dry creekbed conveys the sense of water. The boulders and gravel are placed so as to conjure the idea that the force of water shaped the creekbed. Before you shop for boulders and gravel, study streams in the natural landscape or photographs of streams.

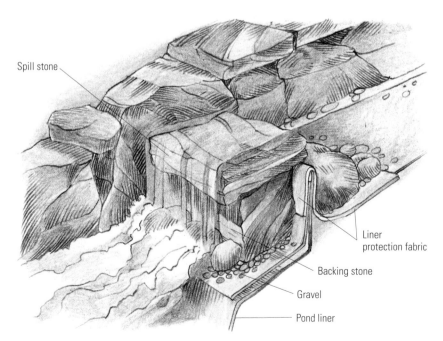

Spill stone

Liner protection fabric

Backing stone

Gravel

Pond liner

Notice how streams widen on bends, turning around a rock promontory and leaving a shallow beach downstream on the outside curve. Boulders too big to roll in the current stay in the middle of the stream, smaller ones wash to the sides, where they lie half-buried in silt. In most streams, there are places where the water slows and pools in deep places, and places where it chuckles over rocky shallow stretches or slips through a gorge. Water always flows in the line of least resistance as it runs over the ground.

To use the creekbed as a drainage channel for seasonal runoff, bury a length of 4-inch perforated drainpipe in the center of the creek (see page 80). Pack gravel under the pipe as necessary so it slopes downhill (a 2 percent grade is sufficient) to a storm drain, well, or pond. You don't need a liner.

BUILDING A STREAM

A stream requires a mild slope, so the water doesn't rush down it too fast; a 1 or 2 percent grade is about right. To make the water flow look natural, see the suggestions for dry creekbeds above.

As you design the source and destination of the stream, consider where the water will collect when the pump is off. A mountain stream might originate from a waterfall, a lowland stream from a bubbling spring (see the pebble fountain, page 100). Both might end naturally and conveniently at a pond; the alternative is to install a reservoir tank that's large enough to hold all the water that drains from the stream.

Excavate the streambed to a depth of 6 inches in the shallow stretches, 10 inches in the occasional deep pools (water will collect here when the pump is turned off). To allow for plants, dig shallow trenches on the side of the streambed, as shown below. Make the streambed wide enough to accommodate rocks and pebbles; placing stones in the stream, rather than just on its edges, helps hide the liner.

Line the excavation with 3 inches of damp sand and a layer of liner protection fabric; then lay the liner and another layer of liner protection fabric. Place stones, gravel, and sand in and along the watercourse. Plant marginal or bog plants in soil in the trenches and cover the soil with gravel or pebbles so the soil doesn't leak into the stream.

Run the stream and experiment with the placement of the rocks until you are pleased with the look of the stream and the sound of the water. Check for leaks. Then finish the edging, disguising the liner with overhanging rocks or a layer of sand or gravel.

DRY FALLS, WET POOL

This dry cascade of rocks above a glittering pool recalls a scene in the mountains in summer. The evidence of the waterfall is in the carefully chosen streaked cliff faces of the stones and the lush plants along the banks that must have grown up in the spray of the spring snow melt.

Because you don't want rainwater running off the dry waterfall into the pond, bury a length of perforated drainpipe in a gravel bed (see page 80) at the foot of the falls. Starting at the pond edge, wedge the first boulder securely back and into the slope. Set the one above it, imagining as you work the course the water would take. Think about the force of the water, the way it might tip boulders against one another. Place stone chips and gravel in the shallow pools between the boulders, and plant diminutive plants in the crevices.

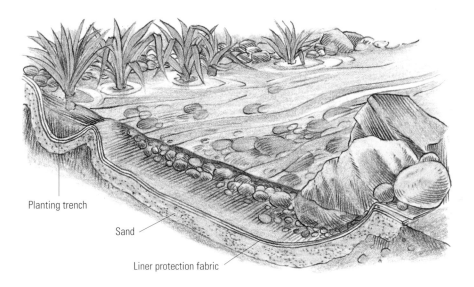

Planting trench

Sand

Liner protection fabric

ROCK GARDENS

Rock gardens range in scale from pockets between paving stones to boulder outcroppings on slopes and mounds that mimic mountain ranges. The simplest gardens couldn't be simpler—a creeping plant through the cracks of a patio. The most ambitious requires an eye that sees the possibilities of vast cliffs in the faces of small rocks.

PLANTING A ROCK GARDEN

To plant a new rock garden, arrange the plants in their pots on top of the soil and then plant each one so that the top of the root ball sits about ½ inch above the soil surface. Once the rock garden is planted, mulch the surface with gravel, spreading it carefully and teasing a little around the crown of each plant, and water well. To add a plant later, first clear the gravel mulch well away from the planting area so it doesn't get mixed or trodden into the soil.

Gravel

PLANTING A PATH OR PATIO

Gravel paths and patios often sprout seedlings that got started by themselves from seeds blowing onto the gravel. Plant annuals and perennials known for their self-seeding characteristics nearby if you like the idea of the gravel being naturally taken over this way. Weed selectively, and water as necessary.

Gaps of 2 inches between paving stones are sufficient for plantings of small, creeping ground covers or bulbs. Fill the spaces with amended topsoil to ½ inch below the tops of the stones. Buy young plants, or tear clumps into small rooted pieces, insert them between the stones, tamp the soil firmly, and water them. See pages 118–119 for a list of suitable plants.

PLANTING A DRY-STONE WALL

Plant a dry-stone wall as you build it. After laying each course of stones, choose the largest gaps and line them and the space behind them with sphagnum moss, which will help to keep the soil in place. Fill the pockets with soil—whichever type of soil the plant prefers—place the plant roots in the soil, tamp the soil in place, and water gently. Spray the plants with water regularly until they are established, then provide water as needed.

Choose plants to suit the microclimate on the wall surface (see the plant list on pages 120–121). The south or west face of a wall is a warm, sunny place; the north or east face, cooler and shadier. Because of the difficulty of watering plants set into a wall, in a dry climate choose plants that will thrive in an arid environment.

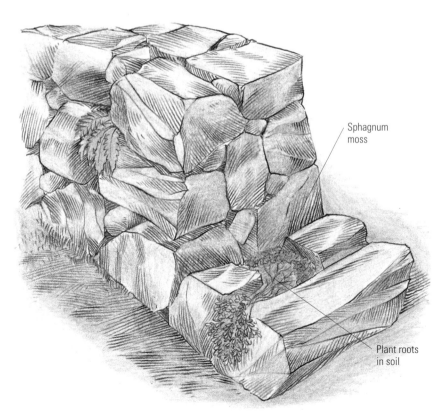
Sphagnum moss

Plant roots in soil

MAKING A ROCKY OUTCROPPING

A natural gentle slope is ideal for an outcropping of boulders. As you design the group and shop for the rock, bear in mind that a range of rock sizes, including one or two large boulders, makes a more effective composition than all small stones; and native stone looks more harmonious than stone brought in from another region.

To mimic a natural outcropping, lay the stones in one or more bands, like strata (see page 93). If the rock has a grain, place the rocks so the grain runs the same way. Place the large boulders first, and scatter the smallest rocks at their feet, as if they had chipped and fallen from the large rocks. Avoid a "raisin-cookie" effect—small rocks dotted about the slope.

See pages 92–93 for directions on how to transport and install the boulders and pages 122–126 for plant suggestions.

MAKING A SCREE

Natural screes are deep piles of fragmented stone that lie at the base of cliffs or on ridges in the mountains; they are the natural homes for alpine and desert plants that need fast-draining soil.

Before you excavate an area for a garden scree, consider how well your soil drains. If your soil is sandy and already fast-draining at all times of the year, you don't need to install the 18 inches of fast-draining scree mixture described below; simply excavate to a depth of 1 inch to lay the crushed stone surface. If your soil drains poorly, build the scree on a mound.

Site the scree on a gentle slope if you have one. Place a group of boulders at the top of the scree area, arranging them like a natural outcropping as shown above right, with their steepest, cliff-like sides facing the scree and the top of each stone tilting at the same angle.

Excavate the scree area to a depth of 18 inches. Pour 4 inches of equal parts gravel and sand into the bottom of the excavation.

Gravel and sand are poured into the excavation first.

Fill the scree to within 1 inch of the surface with a fast-draining soil mix of 1 part crushed rock (½- or ¾-inch minus) or pea gravel, 1 part coarse sand, and 2 parts good fertile garden soil. The exact proportions are not important; some rock gardeners prefer far more rock, but increasing the ratio of rock means the mix will dry out more quickly and you will need to water more often.

Finish the scree by spreading 1 inch of crushed stone on the surface (below right). Choose a stone that matches the color of the boulders for the most natural look.

Choose plants suitable for the scree (see the plant list on pages 122–125), placing only heat-loving plants on a south- or west-facing slope. Although a scree looks stony and dry, because the surface water disappears so fast, natural scree plants receive water most of the year from melting snow or underground springs, so don't forget to water your scree garden during the growing season.

The scree is finished with 1 inch of crushed stone.

A Japanese Mound Garden

A Rock Slab Garden

Making a Mound Garden, or Rockery

The original Japanese rock garden mounds *(koyama)* resemble peaks and foothills and are planted with dwarf conifers, or they are made of sand and designed purely for their sculptural lines. The Western mound garden, or rockery, is usually planted with ground covers and a variety of rock garden or small native plants.

Make the mounds by digging trenches and piling the soil into irregular elongated mounds. Interconnect them with paths if you like. Remove the top soil first and put it to one side, so you can spread it on the top of the finished mounds. Avoid making the mounds too even, too high, or too steep. Tamp the soil as you build.

Place a few rocks on the slopes of the mounds or at the base, being careful not to overdo the amount of rock. To make watering easier and to prevent the plants from sliding down the slopes, install the plants in "foxholes" made of bottomless gallon cans. At the very least, scoop out a foxhole in the slope, form a rim for it with excavated soil, and reinforce the rim with small stones.

Making a Slab Garden

Large rocks that can be split along natural fractures or seams into three or four slabs are ideal for making a natural slab garden. Have the rock yard do the splitting; the rock is much easier to transport in slabs.

Piece the slabs back together in your garden, leaving gaps of a few inches between them for planting. Pack the gaps with gravel and a fast-draining soil mix, and plant a miniaturized landscape with dwarf conifers or succulents and tiny matting ground covers.

Making a Trough Garden

An easy way to start rock gardening is to make a trough garden. On a small scale, you can practice making a miniaturized landscape or growing a small collection of rock plants that have the same soil and light needs. Troughs are also popular among experienced rock gardeners. They display well the tiniest specimen rock plants, which would be lost in a larger garden, and they can be moved, if necessary, to protect sensitive plants from too much summer sun or winter cold.

Choose naturally dwarf plants with small features for your trough; perhaps include at least one plant with a long flowering season. To thrive together, the plants should have the same soil and light preferences. Choose a soil mix to suit your plants. If you are creating a miniaturized landscape, make contours in the soil surface to mimic a natural topography, and place "boulders" the size of pebbles or "screes" of fine gravel.

Trough gardens are more vulnerable to frost than are rock gardens in the ground, and they are more prone to drying out in hot, dry weather. In cold and even moderately mild climates, protect the plants from frost by covering the trough with branches of evergreen shrubs or by moving the trough into an unheated sun porch. Water the trough regularly during summer dry spells.

MAKING A HYPERTUFA TROUGH

As an alternative to buying an expensive old stone trough, consider making one with hypertufa: a mix of cement, peat moss, and vermiculite, which when it's dry looks like weathered, crumbly stone. You'll need a trough-shaped mold, such as a plastic dishpan or a heavy cardboard box, to work with. Wear rubber gloves to protect your hands and a dust mask to prevent particle inhalation. Choose a flat work space where you can leave the completed trough undisturbed while the cement cures. Cover the work surface with a sheet of plastic.

In a wheelbarrow or other large container, mix together 3 parts peat moss, 3 parts vermiculite, and 2 parts portland cement. Three dry quarts of vermiculite, 3 dry quarts of peat moss, and 2 dry quarts of cement will cover a mold made from a 14-inch pot. For a trough more than 2 feet long, add a handful of Fibermesh—a concrete reinforcing agent—to give the mixture more strength. Add just enough water to make the ingredients malleable. Mix them together well.

You can shape the trough using either the inside or the outside of the mold. For a rough exterior and a smooth interior, use the outside of the mold. For a smooth exterior and a rough interior, pat the mixture into the mold's interior.

Place the mold upside down (for a rough exterior) or right side up (for a smooth exterior) on the plastic-covered work surface. Cover the mold with a sheet of plastic, tucking the edges firmly around or beneath the mold. Scoop up a handful of the moistened mixture, and starting at the bottom and working toward the top, press it firmly to the mold, building up a layer about 1½ to 2 inches thick.

Wet your gloves and pat the exposed surface to smooth it. To create drainage holes, insert two or three wood dowel pieces, ¼ inch in diameter and a few inches long, into the trough bottom. Loosely cover the mold with another sheet of plastic and allow the mixture to cure for a week or longer. The slower the cure, the stronger the trough; to slow down the curing process, mist the mixture. Twist the dowels occasionally so they don't stick when you remove them.

After the cement has hardened, remove the plastic cover and carefully slip the trough off the mold. Allow it to set for another week or two to dry completely. Spray the trough with a hose to remove any white lime deposits on the surface. Brush the trough with buttermilk, or yogurt thinned with water to the consistency of buttermilk, to encourage the growth of algae and moss.

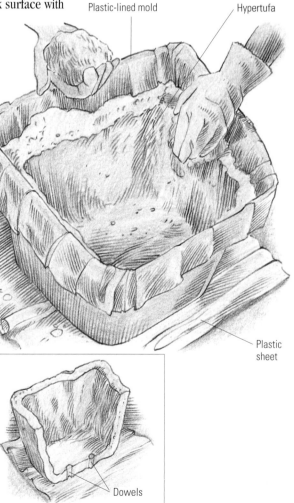

Plastic-lined mold

Hypertufa

Plastic sheet

Dowels

ALPINE
DESERT
BASALT
.22¢ lb.

Shopping for materials for a stone project is outdoor work first. Put on heavy boots and thick leather gloves and perhaps take a camera, a measuring tape, and a notebook. Thus equipped, you'll be able to walk among the giant boulders and flagstone slabs at the rock yard to look for the right-sized pieces with pretty striations or pockets of lichen, and if necessary, take home the notes you'll need to make a final decision.

A GUIDE TO
SHOPPING

Once the stone is in place in your garden, the shopping choices revolve around the soft finishing materials: diminutive, gemlike plants for walls and crevices, tough little creepers for the joints between stepping-stones, and myriad small-scale plants, including dwarf conifers, evergreen shrublets, succulents, and the very tiniest rock plants that make vividly colored, flat carpets for a rocky meadow or scree. Local nurseries usually stock common rock garden plants. For rare or unusual plants, send off for specialty nursery catalogs or contact the North American Rock Garden Society (see page 125 for more information).

This chapter will help you select the stone, tools, and plants you'll need for your stone project. There's also a glossary of stone-building terms here plus e-mail and website addresses of mail-order suppliers of rock garden plants.

Before you buy stone, take the time to study its color—when dry and when wet—the flatness and texture of its surface, and its shape, size, and thickness.

SHOPPING FOR STONE

Knowing what stone is available and selecting the best stone for the project are essential parts of a stoneworker's job. Don't be in a hurry when you shop. Make a scouting tour of the suppliers of stone in your area, and then take your time over your decisions, just as an apprentice stonemason would.

FIRST CHOICE: LOCAL STONE

Local stone is almost always a landscape architect's first choice for any type of stonework—walls, paving, or boulders. It's guaranteed to look right and natural, which are extremely desirable characteristics for a garden feature. Stone imported from another region may look exotic; it can be used effectively close to the house, to complement the color of the house walls or the flooring inside the house, but it's unlikely to fit so easily in the more natural parts of the garden. Be especially careful about choosing colorful stone; try to visualize the effect of a large area of it, bearing in mind that the color is intensified by the scale.

Local stone is usually the least expensive stone available, because transportation costs from the quarry are relatively low. It may also be available in various forms: mechanically crushed gravel, squared blocks for walls and paving, and large and small boulders. You might be able to use just one type of stone for all your stone projects in the garden, which will make your work look even more natural.

Roughly squared stone blocks can be stacked fairly easily into walls or used for paving. For a tight fit, stone needs to be cut precisely.

SELECTING STEPPING-STONES

The most natural-looking stepping-stones have rough, pocked, and mossy surfaces. The stones need not be perfectly flat, especially if the path is in an informal part of the garden where people will be walking slowly. The eye quickly notes an uneven surface, so that if at least several of the stones are uneven, there's not much chance of someone tripping. Avoid stones with indentations in the center of the tread, because if water collects there and freezes, the path will become dangerous. But don't reject a stone just because it has an irregular surface; it's the irregularity in the stones that makes the path interesting.

Large stepping-stones create the most gracious path, and also the most stable. Stones should be at least 18 inches wide and 15 to 18 inches deep, but buy larger ones if you can, including a few up to 3 feet wide. For a raised path, buy stones at least 3 to 4 inches thick.

Flagstone is the most common material for stepping-stones. Large pieces of weathered fieldstone make a particularly natural-looking path, but if your local stone is round, you'll need to bury most of each stone. Although it's usually seen in formal settings, cut stone may be used for stepping-stone paths. Smooth river rocks become too slippery when they're wet.

Measure the length of your path before you shop. If each stone will be 18 inches deep and you've decided on 6-inch gaps between stones (see page 82), then you'll need 1 stone for every 2 feet of your path. It doesn't matter how wide the stones are, 20 inches or 36 inches, because you'll lay the longest side across the path. For a relatively small project, it's worth spending time matching the shapes of the stones, so that they speak to one another (see page 83).

A steel-jawed crane hoists a rock slab into the bed of a truck.

SELECTING GRAVEL

Gravels may be natural—quarried or collected from natural deposits—or manufactured by mechanically crushing large pieces of stone. In either case, the pieces are usually graded to a uniform size, such as ⅝-inch, or ⅝-minus, meaning pieces that are ⅝ of an inch and smaller. The gravel may be washed clean or sold with the finings, the dust from the crushing process that is used to bind the gravel and make it compact well.

Naturally occurring gravel pieces are sometimes varicolored and pretty, but they have rounded edges, which are hard to compress into a firm walking surface. Use rounded gravels for decorative purposes, such as gravel and trough gardens and water features, or for small areas of paving where it doesn't matter so much that your feet sink and drag as if you're walking in a tin of buttons.

For gravel foundations, beneath paths and walls, for example, use crushed rock, because its sharp-edged pieces compact tightly, making a more stable base than rounded gravel, such as pea gravel, which rolls and scatters.

A ⅜-inch gravel is comfortable underfoot. Gravel pieces larger than ¾ inch can be too bumpy, and a very fine gravel can be too dusty. Take home gravel samples and study the color of them, dry and wet, before you make a decision.

Gravel, like sand, is sold by the cubic yard or by the ton. To calculate how much you'll need, multiply in feet the width of the space by the length of it by the depth of the material; then divide the resulting number by 27 to convert it to cubic yards. For example, for a path 6 feet wide and 20 feet long that requires a 2-inch layer of gravel, you'd need 20.4 cubic feet of gravel ($6 \times 20 \times 0.17$), or ¾ of a cubic yard. You might add on an extra 10 percent to be sure you don't run short. A ton of gravel is equal to about 20 cubic feet.

Loose stones and gravel, clockwise from top: quartz, La Paz, ¼-in. dolomite, ¾-in. red lava, tumbled Japanese riverstone, ¼-in. pea gravel, aqua cove mix, 5/16-in. red lava.

SELECTING CUT STONE AND FLAGSTONE

Cut stone and flagstone are available in a wide range of colors, from black slate to shades of buff, gray, and pink limestone, sandstone, and marble, although marble is usually considered too expensive for most garden projects. It's tempting to choose the loveliest stone you can afford, but make sure it's suitable.

Check that the stone color complements the color of your house, garden furniture, and plantings. A neutral gray or brown stone blends in easily; a pink stone is best used in small areas. Study the stone surface. Is it absolutely flat or does it have a little texture and shadow for interest? Is it flat enough as a surface for your outdoor dining furniture? How durable is it? In time will the edges crumble or will the color fade? Is it slippery when wet? Will it stain easily if sticky tree litter or soft berries drop on it, or will it grow mossy in the shade? Sealants are available to help prevent staining, but they can change the color of the stone, and they need to be reapplied regularly. Don't feel hesitant about asking the stone supplier all these questions before you buy.

Cut stone and flagstone are sold by the square foot or by the ton. To calculate how much you'll need in square feet, multiply in feet the width of the

Flagstone, left to right: Boquet Canyon, stardust flagstone, Idaho quartzite, California Mariposa slate.

Flagstone, left to right: Lompoc flagstone, pink Arizona flagstone, chocolate Arizona flagstone, tan Arizona flagstone.

patio or path by the length. The stone supplier will advise you how much stone to order if it sells by the ton. Buy extra stone to allow for breakages; it may be hard to match the stone later. Be aware that the dimensions of a piece of cut stone may vary a little, not every 1-square-foot piece of bluestone, for example, will be cut exactly to size; the variance may be as great as ½ inch. If you are planning to lay cut stone with no gaps between the stones or very small gaps, talk to the supplier before you buy the stone. Some kinds of stones are cut precisely, other kinds are cut more roughly.

For crazy-paving projects (made of pieces of flagstone with irregular edges), select a range of stone sizes. Avoid a preponderance of small pieces, because it'll make the paving look fussy.

Cut stone and flagstone for paving are usually between 1 and 2 inches thick. For the most stable paving surface, select large pieces of thick stone.

SELECTING WALL STONE

There are two choices for wall stone: rubble, usually uncut stone although it may be roughly squared, and ashlar, a neatly trimmed block or slab of stone. Ashlar is the more expensive option, but it's by far the easier to lay. Because it's flat on all sides, you can almost set ashlar in regular courses like brick. If you are mortaring the wall, ashlar will require less mortar than rubble. The most common ashlar stones are sandstone and limestone, because those stones are easy to split and trim.

Rubble for wall work is difficult to cut; the work is extremely slow and chancy, even with precision masonry tools. Consider buying at least 25 percent more stone than you'll need, so that you can search through the pile for a stone that is the right size. "Search more or shape more," stonemasons say.

To make a handsome wall with rubble, buy a variety of sizes of stone. The largest stones should be five times larger than the smallest. As you pick out what you need at the stone yard, bear in mind that flat stone or stone that is naturally blocky will be much easier to work with than rounded stone.

For a dry-stone wall, search for large stones for the foundation course, plenty of long stones for bond stones, and some flat stones to cap the wall. If you have small stones on the site, you can use those to fill in the center of the wall.

Wall stone is usually sold by the ton. Calculate the surface area of your wall by multiplying in feet the height by the length, and when you've chosen the type of stone you want, discuss a suitable order with the stone supplier. The thickness of the stone determines how much you'll need, so amounts may vary greatly depending on what is available.

Suppliers of the modular masonry units for retaining walls provide a chart for calculating how many units you'll need for your wall. Before you leave for the store, measure the wall length and decide on the height.

SELECTING VENEER STONE

Veneer stone is specially cut for veneering concrete block walls. It's a uniform 4- or 6-inch thickness with a flat back that allows for easy installation.

Veneer stone is sold by the ton. To calculate how much you'll need, multiply in feet the height of your wall by the length

Left to right: Sonoma fieldstone, red cinder, Sonoma fieldstone, waterwashed flagstone, Sonoma fieldstone, feather rock, desert cloud, desert paint, imagination stone, holey fieldstone.

of your wall, and discuss a suitable order with your stone supplier. The amount of stone you'll need will vary greatly, depending on the thickness of the stone.

SELECTING BOULDERS

Boulders in the natural landscape have a harmony of texture, color, and line. To achieve a natural look, limit your purchases to one type of rock, and for the most part choose similar rock shapes—all roughly squares or goose eggs or diamonds or domes. One rock with a particularly pleasing line or an angled surface full of light and shadow would make a fine focal point in a meadow or rocky slope, but for a peaceful, natural composition, you don't want every boulder to catch the eye. Before you shop, consider how and where you intend to place the boulders (see page 93).

If you are choosing boulders to make a rock grouping for a Japanese garden, buy sculptural pieces, including perhaps a tall vertical rock, a reclining rock, and several other shapes. Group the rocks like sculpture, each rock in a visually pleasing relationship to the others.

Smooth, river-washed boulders are a natural choice for water features, but buy only one or two of the most beautifully sculpted ones. Too many exquisite rocks, even if naturally shaped, can spoil the harmony of a water garden, drawing the eye away from the water and the plantings. Aim for a visual balance among rock, water, and plants. Some stonemasons prefer fieldstone for water features, because it's less stunning. It's also much less expensive.

GETTING THE STONE HOME

Most stone, even small amounts of it, weighs too much to bring home in the trunk of a car or the back of a small truck. Instead of making dozens of trips, ask the supplier about delivery options. You may be able to rent a dump truck from the supplier for a couple of hours.

Prepare for the delivery. For loose materials, such as gravel and sand, lay down large tarps in the receiving area, so that the material doesn't get trodden into the ground. Organize help to transport your stone to the garden if the supplier delivers only to the curb. You may need special equipment to transport large boulders (see page 93).

SOURCES OF STONE

Home improvement centers usually stock only a small range of stone. For the best local sources, where contractors and landscape architects order materials, check the Yellow Pages under these headings: Building Materials, Landscape Equipment and Supplies, Quarries, Rock, Stone-Natural.

A shopper at the Marenakos quarry, east of Seattle, studies a pile of boulders that weigh between 900 and 1,800 pounds apiece.

TOOLS

Stonework requires some basic safety gear and, to make the work zip along smoothly, the right tools. Shop where the professionals shop and, for large jobs, rent the same power tools they use.

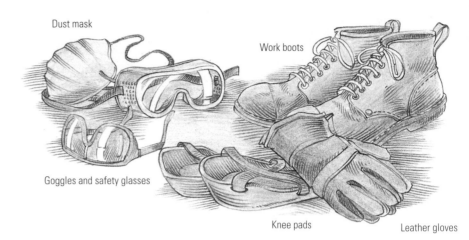

Dust mask

Work boots

Goggles and safety glasses

Knee pads

Leather gloves

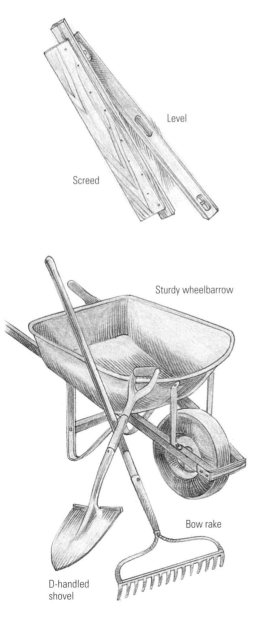

Level

Screed

Sturdy wheelbarrow

Bow rake

D-handled shovel

OUTFITTING YOURSELF SAFELY

DUST MASK. Wear when working with dry portland cement or any dusty material.

EARMUFF HEARING PROTECTORS OR EARPLUGS. Wear when operating power tools for any length of time.

GOGGLES OR SAFETY GLASSES. Wear when working with dry mortar or concrete and when anything could splash or bounce into your eyes, such as when chipping or cutting stone, spreading mortar, or using muriatic solution.

KNEE PADS. Wear for paving jobs, both for comfort and to help prevent damage to knees and clothing.

LEATHER GLOVES. Wear when handling stones and when working with mortar or concrete, dry or wet; tuck sleeves into gloves.

WORK BOOTS. Wear when lifting or carrying stones and when using sharp tools; the steel-toed kind are especially good.

BASIC TOOLS FOR STONE PROJECTS

CARPENTER'S OR MASON'S LEVEL. A level is used to check that a paving surface is flat or that a vertical wall face is plumb. For large areas, a 4- or 6-foot-long level is more practical than a 2-foot-long level. A line level clips onto taut twine and tells you whether the twine is perfectly level.

MASON'S TWINE AND CORNER BLOCKS. Stringing twine carefully around the perimeter of a path or patio will help you keep the paving edges straight; you can also use the twine as a guide for the height of the edging or the finished surface.

MEASURING TAPE. For laying out all but the smallest paths and patios, you'll need a steel measuring tape, 16 or 25 feet long. Choose a 1-inch-wide tape, which doesn't twist or buckle as much as a narrow tape, so that you can extend it easily over longer distances.

METAL BOW RAKE. A metal rake with a bow frame will help you level soil, sand, or gravel.

SCREED. A screed is a handmade leveling tool for a bed of sand or wet concrete. Make one from a length of 2-by-4; nail on a plywood extension that's 3 inches or so shorter on both ends than the 2-by-4 and wider by slightly less than the thickness of the paving unit (see page 87).

Measuring tape

SPADES AND SHOVELS. For excavating, a round-pointed shovel is easy to use, but switch to a straight-edged spade to make the edges of a trench vertical and to square off the trench bottom. A shovel with a short D handle works well for spreading sand and gravel.

STRAIGHTEDGE. To check the level of a large surface, place your level on a straightedge, such as a perfectly straight, long piece of 2-by-4.

TAMPER. Using a hand-held tamper, a heavy metal plate on a pole, you can compact a gravel or sand foundation firmly. A water-fillable roller or a rented power vibrator may also be used for compacting loose materials.

WHEELBARROW. A sturdy wheelbarrow will save you back strain and bruises. For ease of use, distribute loose materials, such as sand and gravel, so that the greatest weight is at the front and try not to transport too much on each trip. To transport a large stone, put the weight at the back of the wheelbarrow, so that the load is more stable and easier to push over uneven ground, or, even better, use a cart with two side wheels.

TOOLS FOR WORKING WITH MORTAR

MASON'S TROWELS. Mason's trowels are available in many sizes and various triangular shapes. Use a broad one for loading and spreading mortar onto stones and a narrow one for filling and finishing joints. You'll find that a short-handled trowel is easier on the wrists.

MORTAR BOX. A mortar box, or a large plastic tub, is handy for mixing mortar. A wheelbarrow may also be used.

MORTAR HOE. A mortar hoe is designed specifically for mixing mortar by hand, but a plain hoe will suffice.

POINTING TOOLS, OR JOINTERS. There are several tools designed for raking out and finishing mortared joints, but a piece of wood or the tip of your trowel will work for most projects.

WIRE BRUSH. A wire brush is a good tool for cleanup. Use it about four hours after spreading the mortar to whisk away the loose crumbs and smooth the joints.

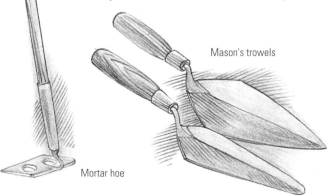

Mason's trowels

Mortar hoe

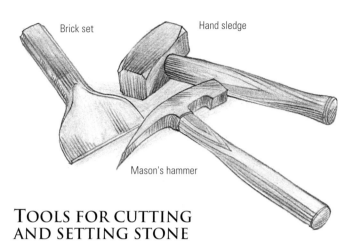

Brick set   Hand sledge

Mason's hammer

TOOLS FOR CUTTING AND SETTING STONE

BATTER GAUGE. A batter gauge helps ensure a proper slope to the faces of a wall. It's another homemade tool constructed for the job at hand (see page 96).

BRICK SET AND HAND SLEDGE. A brick set and hand sledge may be used to trim small amounts of flagstone.

MASON'S HAMMER. With a mason's hammer, you can chip the edge off a stone. For breaking off large pieces of stone or for splitting stones, which is time-consuming and skilled work, stonemasons use a carbide-tipped stone chisel and a sledge, and shims and wedges, and a variety of other, sometimes blacksmith-forged, tools.

PORTABLE SAW. A portable circular saw or grinder with a diamond or masonry blade trims flagstone much faster than you can do it by hand. Don't bother cutting all the way through the stone; if you score to a depth of $3/8$ of an inch on each side, the stone should snap cleanly.

RUBBER MALLET. Just a few taps with a rubber mallet is all that's needed to properly embed a stone paving unit into a bed of sand or mortar.

SPONGE. A good sponge is useful for cleaning stones and wiping off the moisture before you set them in mortar. Check out the tile section of the hardware store for a tiler's sponge, which is what some stonemasons use.

FINDING TOOLS

Your local hardware center or nursery may carry some of the tools you'll need for stonework. Look for the others in outlets that serve contractors or inquire at a tool rental company for equipment you can rent. These places are listed in the Yellow Pages under Building Materials, Contractors' Equipment & Supplies, Rental Service Stores, and Tools.

PLANTS FOR PATHS AND PATIOS

Paths and patios do not need to be bare hardscapes. Numerous types of plants will grow in the cracks between stones or up through gravel and survive the foot traffic. Shop for sturdy plants to go underfoot in the center of the pathway or along the well-worn routes across the patio, and then, if you like, add a few delicate garden plants to your shopping list to set out along the less-trodden areas at the path or patio edges.

Sturdiness is the vital characteristic of a paving plant. The most popular candidates, such as creeping thyme and blue star creeper, can be stepped on regularly and will continue to form a thick, even carpet; they thrive in the heat reflected off the stones and in a meager few inches of soil.

Some of the paving plants in the following chart produce flowers; some plants release a fragrance when stepped on; some make mats as neat and fine as moss, while others grow low but more loosely. Choose a plant that takes at least moderate foot traffic for the center of a path or the main routes across a patio. (If you are building a path of raised stepping-stones, the plants set in the cracks can be more delicate because they won't be trampled on.)

Select plants that make a flat mat, or use no plants at all, for areas where people may be walking at night or walking with gro-ceries. Look for a plant that shows off the beauty of the stone, for example, one with a fall leaf color that matches the striations in the stone; take a sample of stone with you when you shop. Don't be tempted to buy the fastest-growing low ground cover, because you may then spend innumerable hours later clipping it back from covering your stones and rooting it out of neighboring flower beds. A plant that grows thickly, however, will compete well against weeds.

Because of the reflected heat off the stones and the limited amount of soil and water available in the planting spaces, the gaps between stone paving present a formidable environment for new plants. Buy small, young plants and keep them well watered until they are established; in hot weather, erect shade cloth over the plants if you can or mulch light-colored stones with bark. If the plants fail, try sowing seeds in the gaps.

ACAENA BUCHANANII. Sheep bur
0°F/–18°C. ☼ ☼ ◑ ● SUN OR PARTIAL SHADE, BURNS IN HOT SUN, REGULAR WATER. SOME FOOT TRAFFIC.

Gray-green, loose, creeping, fine-textured mat. Remove burrs which form in summer and can stick to clothing and pets.

AJUGA REPTANS. Carpet bugle
0°F/–18°C. ☼ ☼ ● SUN OR PARTIAL SHADE, REGULAR WATER. LIGHT FOOT TRAFFIC.

Quickly spreading mat of dark green leaves 2–3 in. wide, usually blue flowers borne in 4–5-in.-tall spikes in late spring. Varieties with bronze- or metallic-tinted leaves keep color best in sun. Needs good drainage and air circulation. May escape into neighboring beds unless contained.

ARENARIA MONTANA. Sandwort
–20°F/–29°C. ☼ ● SUN, REGULAR WATER. MODERATE FOOT TRAFFIC.

Grayish green mat, 2–4 in. high, with profuse dense mosslike foliage and white flowers in late spring to early summer.

Ajuga reptans

Cerastium tomentosum

BELLIS PERENNIS. English daisy
–20°F/–29°C. ☼ ☼ ● ●● SUN, LIGHT SHADE IN WARM AREAS, MODERATE TO LOTS OF WATER. SOME FOOT TRAFFIC.

Rosettes of dark green leaves, with white-pink flowers—the daisy you see sometimes growing in lawns. Varieties are available with plump, double red or pink flowers.

CERASTIUM TOMENTOSUM. Snow-in-summer
–20°F/–29°C. ☼ ☼ ● SUN, PARTIAL SHADE IN HOT CLIMATES, REGULAR WATER FOR FAST GROWTH. LIGHT FOOT TRAFFIC.

Dense, spreading, tufty mats of silvery gray leaves, 6–8 in. high, with masses of white flowers in early summer. Needs good drainage. Not long-lived.

CHAMAEMELUM NOBILE. Chamomile
–20°F/–29°C. ☼ ☼ ● SUN OR PARTIAL SHADE, MODERATE WATER. MODERATE FOOT TRAFFIC.

Soft, spreading mat of finely cut, aromatic, light bright green leaves, with small yellow buttonlike flowers in summer. 'Treneague' is nonflowering, more compact.

COTULA SQUALIDA.
New Zealand brass buttons
−10°F/−23°C. ☼ ☼ ◗ ◖ SUN OR PARTIAL SHADE,
MODERATE WATER. MODERATE FOOT TRAFFIC.

Creeping plant 2–3 in. tall, with soft, hairy, bronzy green leaves, tiny yellow brass button flowers.

DICHONDRA MICRANTHA
25°F/−4°C. ☼ ☼ ◗ ◖ ◖ SUN OR PARTIAL SHADE,
REGULAR OR HEAVY WATER. MODERATE FOOT TRAFFIC.

Small round leaves like miniature water lily pads, to 6 in. tall in moist shade. Spreads by runners.

HERNIARIA GLABRA. Green carpet
−10°F/−23°C. ☼ ◗ ◖ SUN OR SHADE, REGULAR WATER.
OCCASIONAL FOOT TRAFFIC.

Two- to three-in. tall, with bright green tiny leaves. Rooting stems won't grow out of control.

HIPPOCREPIS COMOSA
−15°F/−26°C. ☼ ◗ ◖ SUN, REGULAR TO MODERATE WATER.
LIGHT FOOT TRAFFIC.

Three-in.-high mat of vetch-like divided leaves, with golden yellow, sweet pea–shaped flowers in spring.

LAURENTIA FLUVIATILIS (PRATIA PEDUNCULATA). Blue star creeper
10°F/−12°C. ☼ ☼ ◗ ◖ SUN, PARTIAL SHADE IN HOT AREAS,
REGULAR WATER. MODERATE FOOT TRAFFIC.

Creeping, spreading plant, 2–3 in. tall, with pointed, oval leaves similar to those of baby's tears. Pale blue, starlike flowers sparkle late spring and summer.

MAZUS REPTANS
−30°F/−34°C. ☼ ☼ ◗ ◖ SUN, PARTIAL SHADE IN HOT AREAS, REGULAR WATER.
LIGHT FOOT TRAFFIC.

Slender stems creep and root along ground, sending up bright green leafy branches 1–2 in. tall. Produces purplish blue flowers in spring and early summer. Needs rich soil. Freezes to ground in cold climates. White-flowering form available.

MENTHA REQUIENII. Jewel mint of Corsica
0°F/−18°C. ☼ ☼ ◗ ◖ SUN OR PARTIAL SHADE, REGULAR WATER.
SOME FOOT TRAFFIC.

Creeping, fragrant mat, ½ in. high; has bright green mossy effect. Tiny light purple flowers in summer. Disappears during winter in colder areas. Spreads by underground stems; can be invasive.

PHYLA NODIFLORA. Lippia
25°F/−4°C. ☼ ◖ ◖ SUN, REGULAR TO LITTLE WATER. MODERATE FOOT TRAFFIC.

Gray-green mat, with small lilac to rose flowers from spring through fall that attract bees. Dormant during winter.

RAOULIA AUSTRALIS
5°F/−15°C. ☼ ◖ SUN, MODERATE WATER. VERY LIGHT FOOT TRAFFIC.

Very close mat of small gray leaves, with inconspicuous pale yellow flowers in spring. Needs sandy soil, perfect drainage.

Chamaemelum nobile

Soleirolia soleirolii

Thymus praecox arcticus

SAGINA SUBULATA. Irish moss
−20°F/−29°C. ☼ ◗ ◖ ◖ SUN OR PARTIAL SHADE,
REGULAR WATER. MODERATE FOOT TRAFFIC.

Dense mosslike mass, sometimes humping with age. Needs good soil, good drainage, occasional feeding. Scotch moss, *S. s.* 'Aurea', is a golden green form.

SOLEIROLIA SOLEIROLII. Baby's tears
9°F/−13°C. ☼ ◖ ◖ PARTIAL OR FULL SHADE, REGULAR WATER, WILL TOLERATE SOME ARIDITY. OCCASIONAL FOOT TRAFFIC.

Lush, neat, medium green mat, 1–4 in. high, freezes to mush in hard frosts but comes back. Roots easily from pieces of stem and can be invasive.

THYMUS PRAECOX ARCTICUS (T. SERPYLLUM). Creeping thyme
−10°F/−23°C. ☼ ☼ ◗ ◖ SUN, OR PARTIAL SHADE IN HOTTEST AREAS, MODERATE WATER. LIGHT FOOT TRAFFIC.

Soft, fragrant, dark green mat of creeping branches 2–6 in. high, with small purplish white flowers in summer. Many cultivars with white, pink, red, or lilac flowers, some with gray leaves.

THYMUS PSEUDOLANUGINOSUS.
Woolly thyme
0°F/−18°C. ☼ ☼ ◗ ◖ SUN, PARTIAL SHADE IN HOTTEST AREAS, MODERATE WATER. LIGHT TO MODERATE FOOT TRAFFIC.

Flat to undulating gray woolly mat, 2–3 in. high, with rarely seen midsummer bloom of tiny pinkish flowers in leaf joints. 'Hall's Woolly' is not as furry but blooms more heavily.

VERONICA REPENS
−20°F/−29°C. ☼ ◗ ◖ SUN OR SOME SHADE, REGULAR WATER.
MODERATE FOOT TRAFFIC.

Shiny green, ½-in.-long leaves on prostrate stems, with tiny lavender to white flowers in spring.

VINCA MINOR. Dwarf periwinkle
−20°F/−29°C. ☼ ◖ ◖ PARTIAL OR FULL SHADE, MODERATE WATER.
HEAVY FOOT TRAFFIC.

Arching stems, to 6 in. high, root where they touch the ground. Shiny dark green leaves, with lavender blue, pinwheel-shaped flowers in spring. Many varieties available, including ones with cream-edged leaves, white or deep purple flowers.

VIOLA LABRADORICA. Violet
−40°F/−40°C. ◖ ◖ SHADE, REGULAR WATER. OCCASIONAL FOOT TRAFFIC.

A tiny violet, 3 in. high or less, with purple-tinged leaves and lavender blue flowers in spring. Can spread aggressively.

ZOYSIA TENUIFOLIA. Korean grass
30°F/−1°C. ☼ ☼ ○ ◖ SUN, TOLERATES SOME SHADE, LITTLE TO REGULAR WATER. MODERATE FOOT TRAFFIC.

Creeping, fine-textured, bumpy grass; spreads slowly. Gives a mossy Oriental look.

PLANTS FOR WALLS AND CREVICES

There are two kinds of walls and plants suitable for each. A utilitarian retaining wall that's not pleasant to look at can be draped with a curtain of foliage until almost no wall shows through the green. A handsome dry-stone wall, on the other hand, needs just a few small plants tucked in here and there to enhance the stonework.

Mask an ugly retaining wall by planting the ground above it with tough, large-spreading evergreen plants such as the following: *Arctostaphylos uva-ursi, Ceanothus gloriosus, Cedrus deodara* 'Pendula', *Cotoneaster dammeri, Euonymus fortunei, Hedera, Juniperus* (prostrate forms), *Lathyrus latifolius, Rosmarinus officinalis* (prostrate forms), or *Vinca.*

The following list describes some of the many smaller plants that grow well in dry-stone wall crevices. The choice is large; the majority of the thousands of species of collectors' rock plants grow readily in dry-stone walls, because their crowns stay dry, sitting between stones, and the air circulation is good, which helps prevent crown rot. The plants are so beautiful that it's tempting to cover a wall entirely with them, but a plant tufting here and there shows the wall and the plants to best advantage.

Most of the plants in the chart prefer sunny or lightly shaded locations; if you have a very shady wall, consider displaying a collection of small ferns there.

Don't let weeds get a foothold in your wall; they are difficult to remove without also pulling out a desirable plant and the precious soil. Pinch weeds out when they're still young.

AETHIONEMA. Stonecress
–20°F/–29°C. ☼ ◕ ◔ SUN, MODERATE TO LITTLE WATER.

Choice shrublets with long clusters of pink flowers on spiky stems in late spring to summer. Grows best in light, porous soil with considerable lime. Deadhead flowers for best bloom. *A. warleyense* (*A.* 'Warley Rose') is neat, compact hybrid, to 8 in. high, planted widely in warmer climates. *A. schistosum*, 5–10 in. high, has slate blue leaves and fragrant, rose-colored flowers.

ARABIS. Rockcress
–20°F/–29°C. ☼ ◕ SUN, MODERATE WATER.

A. caucasica is dependable old favorite for stone walls. Forms mat of gray leaves to 6 in. high. White flowers almost cover plant in early spring. Provide some shade in hot climates. Short-lived where winters are warm and summers humid. *A. sturii* is harder to find but considered one of the finest rock plants. Produces dense, fist-size cushions of small bright green leaves that eventually form small mats and clusters of white flowers on 2–3-in. stems.

ARENARIA MONTANA. Sandwort. See page 118

ARMERIA. Thrift, Sea pink
–20°F/–29°C. ☼ ◕ ◒ SUN, REGULAR TO LITTLE WATER.

Sturdy, tidy mounds of grassy leaves. White, pink, rose, or red flowers in dense globes bloom on stems above foliage from early spring to late fall. *A. maritima* is the most common species; blooms almost all year in some areas. *A. juniperifolia* has tiny, ½-in.-long leaves and 2-in. flower stems; is very touchy about drainage.

AUBRIETA DELTOIDEA. Common aubrieta
–5°F/–21°C. ☼ ◔ ◕ SUN OR LIGHT SHADE, NEEDS WATER BEFORE AND DURING BLOOM.

Forms low, spreading mat, 2–6 in. high, 1–1½ ft. across. Small gray-green leaves. Tiny rose to deep red, pale to deep lilac, or purple flowers. 'Novalis Blue' is a fine seed-grown variety. Short-lived, especially in warm, humid areas.

AURINIA SAXATILIS. Basket-of-gold
–30°F/–34°C. ☼ ◔ ◕ SUN OR LIGHT SHADE, MODERATE WATER.

Dense clusters of tiny golden yellow flowers in spring and early summer. Stems 8–12 in. high, leaves gray. 'Citrina' ('Lutea') has pale yellow flowers, 'Sunnyborder Apricot' has apricot-shaded flowers. Self-sows readily.

CAMPANULA PORTENSCHLAGIANA.
Dalmatian bellflower. See page 123

CERASTIUM TOMENTOSUM. Snow-in-summer.
See page 118

DIANTHUS GRATIANOPOLITANUS. Cheddar pink
–30°F/–34°C. ☼ ◔ ◕ SUN, LIGHT AFTERNOON SHADE IN HOT AREAS, REGULAR WATER.

Neat, compact mound of blue-gray to green-gray foliage on weak, branching stems to 1 ft. long. Very fragrant, typically pink to rose flowers on stems 9–12 in. high. Blooms from spring to fall if flowers are deadheaded. Performs well in the South.

DRYAS OCTOPETALA

–40°F/–40°C. ☀ 💧 SUN, MODERATE WATER.

Carpet of leafy, creeping stems, 2–3 ft. high. Forms erect, white, strawberrylike flowers, 1½ in. across, in late spring through summer. Silvery-tailed seed capsules are as ornamental as flowers.

ERIGERON KARVINSKIANUS.
Mexican daisy, Santa Barbara daisy

–5°F/–21°C. ☀ ☀ 💧 SUN OR LIGHT SHADE, MODERATE WATER.

Graceful trailing plant 10–20 in. high, with multitudes of white-pink daisylike flowers from early summer into fall. Invasive unless controlled. 'Moerheimii' is more compact, with lavender-tinted flowers.

EUPHORBIA MYRSINITES

0°F/–18°C. ☀ 💧💧 SUN, REGULAR TO MODERATE WATER.

Stiff, blue-gray leaves closely set on trailing stems, 8–12 in. high. Flattish clusters of chartreuse to yellow flowers in late winter, early spring. Short-lived in warm-winter areas.

GERANIUM. SMALL SPECIES. Cranesbill

–10°F/–23°C. ☀ ☀ 💧 SUN, AFTERNOON SHADE IN HOT-SUMMER AREAS, REGULAR WATER.

G. cinereum 'Ballerina', to 6 in. tall and much wider, has deeply cut leaves; its lilac pink flowers with purple veining bloom over a long summer season. *G. dalmaticum*, to 6 in. tall, has bright pink flowers in spring and glossy, finely cut leaves. *G. sanguineum striatum* grows 6–12 in. tall, its light pink flowers are heavily veined with red; blooms from late spring well into summer.

GYPSOPHILA REPENS

–20°F/–29°C. ☀ 💧 SUN, MODERATE WATER.

Alpine native with clusters of small white or pink flowers in summer. Grows 6–9 in. high, with trailing stems 1½ ft. long. Leaves blue-green; few when plant is in bloom. White-flowered 'Alba' and pink-flowered 'Dubai' and 'Rosea' are 4 in. high; pink-blossomed 'Dorothy Teacher' is 2 in. high.

HELIANTHEMUM NUMMULARIUM. Sunrose

–20°F/–29°C. ☀ 💧 SUN, MODERATE WATER.

Spreads to 3 ft. across, 6–8 in. high. Number of forms and hybrids between this species and others. Leaves may be glossy green or gray. Clusters of single or double flowers in bright or pastel colors—flame red, apricot, orange, yellow, pink, rose, peach, salmon, or white. Blooms late spring to early summer.

HYPERICUM. LOW-GROWING SPECIES.
St. Johnswort. See also *H. coris*, page 123

10°F/–12°C. ☀ ☀ 💧💧 SUN, PARTIAL SHADE IN HOT AREAS, REGULAR TO MODERATE WATER.

H. reptans is very low-growing, produces large yellow flowers in summer; stems may root along wall.

Armeria maritima

Helianthemum nummularium

Sempervivum tectorum

IBERIS SEMPERVIRENS.
Evergreen candytuft

–20°F/–29°C. ☀ 💧 SUN, REGULAR WATER.

Grows 8–12 in. high and about as wide. Blooms from early spring to summer; pure white flower clusters carried on stems long enough to cut for bouquets. Narrow, shiny dark green leaves are good-looking all year. Many lower-growing, more compact varieties.

LEWISIA

0°F/–18°C. ☀ ☀ 💧 SUN OR LIGHT SHADE, LIGHT WATERING.

Need excellent drainage; plant with fine gravel around crowns to prevent rot. *L. cotyledon* produces rosettes of narrow, fleshy, evergreen leaves and extremely showy clusters of white or pink flowers striped with rose or red on 10-in. stems, in spring to early summer. *L. tweedyi* has stunning, big, satiny salmon pink flowers.

PHLOX SUBULATA. Moss pink

–30°F/–34°C. ☀ ☀ 💧 SUN OR LIGHT SHADE, MODERATE WATER.

Mat, to 6 in. high, of stiffish, needlelike, evergreen to semievergreen leaves on creeping stems. Late spring or early summer flowers that range in color from white through pink to rose and lavender blue. 'Tamanonagalei' ('Candy Stripe') has rose pink blossoms edged in white, reblooms in fall, and is more drought tolerant than the species.

SAPONARIA OCYMOIDES

–20°F/–29°C. 💧 💧💧 SUN, REGULAR TO MODERATE WATER.

To 1 ft. high and 3 ft. across. Oval, dark green leaves. In spring, plant is covered with small pink flowers shaped much like those of phlox. Doesn't tolerate hot, humid summers.

SEDUM ACRE. Goldmoss sedum

0°F/–18°C. ☀ ☀ 💧 ◯ SUN OR LIGHT SHADE, MODERATE TO LITTLE WATER.

To 2–5 in. tall, with upright branchlets from trailing, rooting stems. Tiny light green leaves; yellow flowers in spring. Can become invasive.

SEMPERVIVUM. Houseleek

–20°F/–29°C. ☀ 💧 ◯ SUN, REGULAR TO LITTLE WATER.

Tightly packed rosettes of leaves, with little offsets around parent rosette. Star-shaped flowers in summer. Need good drainage. Many species, including *S. tectorum*, hen and chickens, with gray-green rosettes, red or reddish flowers; easy to grow.

THYMUS. Thyme

HARDINESS VARIES. ☀ ☀ 💧 SUN, PARTIAL SHADE IN HOT AREAS, MODERATE WATER.

Heavily scented leaves and masses of little flowers in late spring or summer. Attractive to bees. *T. praecox arcticus*, creeping thyme (–10°F/–23°C), 2–6 in. high, has dark green leaves, small purplish white flowers in summer; *T. pseudolanuginosus*, woolly thyme (0°F/–18°C), reaches 2–3 in. high, with small, woolly, gray leaves.

Plants for Meadows and Screes

The meadow and scree areas of a rock garden provide the most space for growing plants. In the open areas between boulders or on a fan of gravel spilling down a slope, you can create vast-looking carpets of color using a range of plants: true alpines and saxatiles, the plants native to mountain elevations; mat- or small mound-forming perennials and wildflowers; miniature bulbs; and even dwarf, slow-growing shrubs, or shrublets, and small-scale rhododendrons.

The plants listed below range from true alpines, which you'll most likely find in mail-order rock garden catalogs, to common perennials, which are available in most local nurseries. They share only one characteristic: they are small or low growing, with diminutive features except for their flowers. Most require a sunny open location and good drainage. A few will grow happily in the shade of boulders or in a moist spot where rainwater collects or drips from the stone.

ACHILLEA, LOW-GROWING ONES. Yarrow
–30°F/–34°C. ☼ ◑ Sun, MODERATE WATER.

Carefree, generously blooming perennial for summer and fall. Leaves usually finely divided; flower heads in flattish clusters. *A. ageratifolia* (Greek yarrow) makes low mat of silvery leaves, with white flowers on stems 4–10 in. tall. *A. clavennae* (Silvery yarrow) has silvery gray, silky leaves, lobed like chrysanthemum leaves, and ivory white flowers on 5–10-in.-high stems; also sold as *A. argentea*. *A. kellereri* has gray-green ferny leaves, with daisylike, tiny, white flowers with yellow centers; grows to 6 in. tall.

AJUGA. Carpet bugle
0°F/–18°C. ☼ ◑ ◔ Sun OR PARTIAL SHADE, REGULAR WATER.

Several species; all bloom spring to early summer. *A. genevensis* has grayish, hairy stems and coarse-toothed leaves with blue flower spikes; grows 5–14 in. high. *A. pyramidalis* has roundish leaves and violet blue flowers that are inconspicuous among the leaves; grows 2–10 in. tall; 'Metallica Crispa' has reddish brown leaves with a metallic glint. *A. reptans* is the popular ground cover; it spreads quickly by runners and may need to be contained; makes mat of dark green leaves with 4–5-in.-high flower spikes, usually blue; many varieties available, some with bronze- or metallic-tinted leaves.

ANDROSACE. Rock jasmine
0°F/–18°C. ☼ ◔ Sun, MODERATE WATER.

Choice rock garden miniatures with summer flowers. Require perfect drainage, so well suited to screes and gravelly banks. Rarely succeed in warm-winter areas. Many species available from specialists. *A. lanuginosa* forms mats 3 ft. across; leaves are silvery and covered with silky white hairs; primrose-like flowers are pink, on 2-in. stems. *A. primuloides* makes hairy, silvery rosettes, that spread by 4-in.-long runners; flowers are pink, on 5-in. stems.

ANEMONE BLANDA. Windflower
–10°F/–23°C. ☼ ◔ PARTIAL SHADE, REGULAR WATER.

Stems rise 2–8 in. from tuberous roots. Finely divided leaves are covered with soft hairs. In spring, one sky blue flower, 1–1½ in. across, on each stem.

AQUILEGIA, DWARF TYPES. Columbine
–20°F/–29°C. ☼ ◑ ◔ Sun OR FILTERED SHADE, REGULAR WATER.

Columbines have fairylike, woodland quality with their lacy, divided leaves and spur-shaped flowers on slender stems. Bloom spring and early summer; flowers attract hummingbirds. Not long-lived. The native alpine species, *A. alpina*, grows 1–2 ft. tall, with nodding, bright blue flowers to 2 in. across.

ASTER, SMALL TYPES
HARDINESS VARIES. ☼ ◔ Sun, REGULAR WATER.

There are more than 600 species of asters, including many low-growing ones suitable for a rock garden. Bloom is usually late summer to early fall. *A. alpinus* (–30°F/–34°C) makes a 6–12-in.-tall tufty mound, with violet blue flowers 1½–2 in. across in late spring to early summer. *A. frikartii* (–20°F/–29°C) has open, spreading growth to 2 ft. high, and abundant clear lavender to violet blue flowers 2½ in. across in early summer to fall. *A. yunnanensis* 'Napsbury' (–10°F/–23°C) produces dark green leaves in basal tufts. Stems to 1½ ft., each bearing a single lavender blue, orange-centered flower in summer.

CALLUNA VULGARIS, DWARF TYPES. Scotch heather
–20°F/–29°C. ☼ ◔ Sun, REGULAR WATER.

Evergreen shrubs with crowded, tiny leaves and one-sided spikes of bell-shaped flowers. Many dwarf ground cover and rock garden varieties available ranging from 2 in. to 3 ft. tall. Flower colors include white, pale to deep pink, lavender, and purple. Foliage—paler and

deeper greens, yellow, chartreuse, gray, or russet—
often changes color in winter. Most bloom in mid- to
late summer; a few bloom into late fall. Thrive in cool,
moist climates; languish in heat.

CAMPANULA. Bellflower
–30°F/–34°C, EXCEPT AS NOTED. ☼ ◐ ◑ PARTIAL SHADE,
TOLERATE SUN IN COOLEST AREAS, REGULAR TO MODERATE
WATER.

Many species, including gemlike miniature plants and
trailing ground covers. Grow best in cooler climates.
C. carpatica (Tussock bellflower) makes compact,
leafy tufts usually about 8 in. tall, may reach 1–1½ ft.;
leaves are bright green; late spring flowers are blue or
white, open bell- or cup-shaped; easily grown from seed.
C. cochleariifolia (Fairy's thimble), –10°F/–23°C, is a
vigorous, spreading plant, with underground runners;
blooms in summer on wiry stems 6 in. tall; flowers are
dainty, nodding, blue thimbles. *C. portenschlagiana*
(Dalmatian bellflower), –20°F/–29°C, makes
low, leafy mat 4–7 in. high, with roundish deep
green leaves and flaring bell-shaped, violet blue
flowers late spring into summer; spreads moderately fast but not invasive. *C. poscharskyana* (Serbian
bellflower) is very vigorous and needs little water;
star-shaped blue-lilac or lavender flowers bloom
spring to early summer on 1-ft. tall or taller stems.
C. rotundifolia, Bluebell of Scotland or Harebell
(–20°F/–29°C), grows 6–20 in. tall, upright or
spreading; produces broad, bell-shaped, bright blue
summer flowers; flower color is variable, sometimes
in lavender, purple, or white shades.

COTONEASTER
HARDINESS VARIES. ☼ ◑ SUN, MODERATE WATER.

Evergreen shrubs with bright red fruit. *C. congestus,*
Pyrenees cotoneaster (0°F/–18°C), grows slowly to 3
ft. with dense, downward-curving branches, tiny dark
green leaves. *C. dammeri,* bearberry cotoneaster,
(–10°F/–23°C), grows well in sun or partial shade; fast prostrate
growth 3–6 in. tall, 10 ft. wide; branches root along ground; leaves are
bright, glossy green; many varieties available.

CROCUS
–20°F/–29°C. ☼ ◑ ◑ SUN OR PARTIAL SHADE, REGULAR WATER DURING
GROWTH AND BLOOM.

Many species of this bulb besides the familiar *C. vernus* (Dutch cro-
cus). Most bloom in late winter or earliest spring, some bloom in fall.
Mass them for best effect. Won't naturalize where winters are warm.

ERICA CARNEA. Heath
–10°F/–23°C. ☼ ◑ SUN EXCEPT IN HOTTEST CLIMATES, CONSISTENT,
CAREFUL WATERING.

Upright branchlets rise 6–16 in. from prostrate main branches. Small,
needlelike, medium green leaves; produces rosy red flowers in winter

Anemone blanda

Campanula poscharskyana

*Campanula
portenschlagiana*

Erica carnea

and spring. Needs excellent drainage. Unlike most
heaths, tolerates neutral or slightly alkaline soils.
Prune every year.

GALANTHUS NIVALIS.
Common snowdrop
–20°F/–29°C. ☼ ◑ ◑ SUN OR PARTIAL SHADE, REGULAR
WATER DURING GROWTH AND BLOOM.

Dainty white bulb with nodding, bell-shaped blossoms, one per stalk, in early spring. Best adapted to
cold climates.

GENISTA PILOSA. Broom
–10°F/–23°C. ☼ ◑ ○ SUN, MODERATE TO LITTLE WATER.

Fairly fast-growing deciduous shrub, reaching 1–1½
ft. tall with 7-ft. spread. Intricately branched, gray-
green twigs. Sweet pea–shaped, yellow blooms in
spring. Will not run wild. 'Vancouver Gold' is best
selection.

HYPERICUM CORIS. St. Johnswort
10°F/–12°C. ☼ ◑ ◑ ◑ SUN, PARTIAL SHADE IN HOT
AREAS, REGULAR TO MODERATE WATER.

Evergreen shrublet to 6–12 in. tall or taller. Whorls of
narrow, fresh green leaves. Yellow flowers resemble single roses with prominent sunburst of stamens in center;
appear in loose clusters, spring or early summer.

IRIS, SMALL TYPES
–20°F/–29°C, EXCEPT AS NOTED. EXPOSURE NEEDS VARY
BY SPECIES, WATER NEEDS VARY BY SPECIES.

Pacific Coast irises (0°F/–18°C) make clumps like
coarse grass; slender flower stems grow 8 in.–2 ft.,
depending on variety; need sun to light shade, moderate to scant water in summer. Reticulata irises are the
classic rock garden irises; flowers appear on 6–8-in.
stems from bulbs in early spring; leaves appear after
flowers; plant in sunny location, need regular moisture from fall through spring and a dry period during
summer. *I. cristata* has white, lavender, or light blue flowers with
golden crests; leaves are 4–6 in. long; the slender, greenish rhizomes
spread freely; give light shade, regular water.

NARCISSUS, SMALL AND MINIATURE TYPES. Daffodil
HARDINESS VARIES. ☼ ◑ SUN, REGULAR WATER DURING GROWTH AND BLOOM.

N. bulbocodium (Hoop petticoat daffodil), –10°F/–23°C, grows to
6 in. tall, with little, upward-facing flowers that are mostly trumpet;
petals, or segments, are very narrow, pointed; deep and pale yellow varieties available. *N. cyclamineus,* –10°F/–23°C, has backward-curved
lemon yellow segments and narrow, tubular golden cup; grows to 6 in.
high. *N. jonquilla* (Jonquil), –20°F/–29°C, produces clusters of early,
very fragrant golden yellow flowers with short cups; leaves are cylindri-
cal, rushlike. *N. triandrus* (Angel's tears), –20°F/–29°C, also has
rushlike foliage; clusters of small white or pale yellow flowers with short
cups bloom on stems to 10 in. high.

OENOTHERA MACROCARPA. Evening primrose
−10°F/−23°C. ☀ ⬤ SUN, MODERATE WATER.

Prostrate, sprawling stems to 10 in. long. Soft, velvety, 5-in. leaves. Bright yellow, 3–5-in.-wide flowers in late spring and summer; flowers open in afternoon, close following morning. Large, winged seedpods follow the flowers. Also sold as *O. missouriensis*.

PAPAVER ALPINUM. Alpine poppy
−10°F/−23°C. ☀ ⬤ ⬤ SUN, REGULAR TO MODERATE WATER.

Low clump of delicate, blue-green divided leaves. Spring flowers, 1–1½ in. across, open on 5–8-in.-high flower stalks above the foliage; the flower color range is white, orange, yellow, and salmon. Blooms first year from seed sown in fall or early spring. Best adapted to colder climates. Also sold as *P. burseri*.

PENSTEMON, SMALL TYPES
HARDINESS VARIES. ☀ ◑ ⬤ ⬤ SUN, AFTERNOON SHADE IN HOT CLIMATES, REGULAR TO MODERATE WATER.

Large genus of perennials, evergreen shrubs, and shrublets, including many small plants for rock garden. All have tubular flowers attractive to hummingbirds. *P. ambiguus* (Prairie penstemon, Sand penstemon), −30°F/−34°C, is a shrubby perennial; grows to 2 ft. high, with very narrow leaves and broad clusters of white to pink phloxlike flowers; blooms early summer to early fall. *P. centranthifolius*, Scarlet bugler (−20°F/−7°C), is a shrub; it has gray foliage and bright red flame flowers; grows 1–3 feet tall. *P. heterophyllus purdyi*, a perennial hardy to 20°F/−7°C, produces upright or spreading stems, 1–2 ft. high; narrow, pointed leaves; blooms spring to early summer, bearing spikelike clusters of flowers ranging from rosy lavender to intense gentian blue. *P. pinifolius*, 10°F/−12°C, is a spreading shrublet, 4–6 in. high, with crowded needlelike leaves; coral to scarlet flowers, 1½ in. long, appear in summer.

PHLOX, DWARF TYPES
HARDINESS VARIES. ☀ ◑ ⬤ SUN OR LIGHT SHADE, REGULAR WATER, EXCEPT AS NOTED.

See also *P. subulata* (Moss pink) on page 121. All have showy flower clusters. *P. bifida* (Sand phlox), −10°F/−23°C, forms clumps 8–10 in. tall, with narrow, light green leaves; blooms profusely in spring to early summer, bearing lavender to white flowers with deeply notched petals; likes sun, excellent drainage; is drought tolerant. *P. divaricata* (Sweet William phlox), −20°F/−29°C, grows to 1 ft. high, with slender, leafy stems and creeping underground shoots; blooms in spring, bearing open clusters of somewhat fragrant blossoms in pale blue (sometimes with pinkish tones) varying to white; needs light shade. *P. nivalis* (Trailing phlox), −10°F/−23°C, forms loose, 4–6-in.-high mats of narrow leaves; produces pink or white flowers in fairly large clusters, late spring to early summer. *P. stolonifera* (Creeping phlox), −20°F/−29°C, is a

creeping, mounding plant to 6–8 in. high with narrow evergreen leaves; produces profusion of lavender flowers in spring.

POTENTILLA FRUTICOSA 'SUTTER'S GOLD'
−30°F/−34°C. ☀ ◑ ⬤ SUN, SOME SHADE IN HOT CLIMATES, MODERATE WATER.

Deciduous shrub to 1 ft. high, spreading to 3 ft. wide. Blooms from late spring to early fall, bearing clear yellow, roselike flowers 1 in. across.

POTENTILLA RECTA 'WARRENII'
−20°F/−29°C. ☀ ◑ ⬤ SUN, SOME SHADE IN HOT CLIMATES, MODERATE WATER.

Evergreen perennial to 15 in. tall. Profuse show of bright yellow, 1-in. flowers in late spring; strawberry-like foliage.

PRIMULA. Primrose
−10°F/−23°C, EXCEPT AS NOTED. ☀ ☀ ⬤ FILTERED SHADE, TOLERATE SUN IN COOL CLIMATES, REGULAR WATER.

Rhododendron 'Ginny Gee'

Hundreds of species, hybrids, and selections. *P. juliae* hybrids (Juliana primrose) have bright green leaves in tuftlike rosettes; very early flowers—white, blue, yellow, orange-red, pink, or purple—are borne singly or in clusters on 3–4-in. stems. *P. veris* (Cowslip) has charming, fragrant, bright yellow flowers in early spring, on stems 4–8 in. high. *P. vulgaris* (English primrose), 0°F/−18°C, comes in wide range of flower colors, including red, blue, bronze, brown, and wine; double varieties are available.

Rhododendron 'Patty Bee'

PULSATILLA VULGARIS. Pasque flower
−10°F/−23°C. ☀ ◑ ⬤ SUN OR LIGHT SHADE, REGULAR WATER.

Very finely cut, silky-haired leaves. Each stem topped in spring by a cup-shaped flower, 1½ to nearly 4 in. across, silky haired on outer surfaces and centered with a yellow button of stamens. Flower color ranges from white through pink to bluish purple and red. Fluffy seed clusters almost as showy as flowers. Best adapted to cool, moist climates. Also sold as *Anemone pulsatilla*.

Rhododendron 'Ramapo'

RHODODENDRON
HARDINESS VARIES. ◑ ☀ ⬤ BEST IN FILTERED SHADE, SUN IN COOL-SUMMER AREAS, CONSTANTLY MOIST SOIL AND HUMID AIR.

Huge group of plants, including azaleas. Need acid soil that is also moisture-retentive. *R. chryseum*, −10°F/−23°C, is a densely branched dwarf (to 1 ft. tall) plant with small leaves; early spring flowers are small, bright yellow bells, 4 or 5 to a cluster. *R.* 'Ginny Gee', 0°F/−18°C, is a striking, 2-ft. plant with small leaves, dense growth; it's covered with small flowers in midspring; blooms range from pink to white, with striped and dappled patterns. *R. moupinense*, 0°F/−18°C, grows to 1½ ft. tall, has open, spreading habit; small oval leaves are deep red when new, then mature to green; white or pink flowers, spotted red;

Zauschneria californica

blooms in winter. *R.* 'Patty Bee', −10°F/−23°C, makes dense mound to 1½ ft. tall; small leaves give plant a fine-textured look; trumpet-shaped yellow flowers cover plant in midspring. *R.* 'Ramapo', −20°F/−29°C, has dense, spreading growth to 2 ft. in sun, taller in shade; new growth is dusty blue-green; profuse violet blue flowers midspring. *R.* 'Sapphire', −50°F/−46°C, is a twiggy, rounded, dense shrublet to 1½ ft. tall, with tiny gray-green leaves; flowers are small, bright blue, azalealike. The dwarf type Satsuki azaleas, 5°F/−15°C, grow low; many are pendent; large flowers come late.

SEDUM. Stonecrop
0°F/−18°C, EXCEPT AS NOTED. ☼ ◑ ◕ ○ SUN OR LIGHT SHADE, MODERATE TO LITTLE WATER.

Succulents, many small species suitable for rock gardens. *S. brevifolium,* −10°F/−12°C, is a tiny, slowly spreading plant to 2–3 in. high; leaves are gray-white flushed with red; pinkish or white summer flowers. *S. dasyphyllum,* 10°F/−12°C, makes a low, spreading mat of tiny gray-green leaves; small white flowers with pink streaks; needs partial shade. *S. kamtschaticum* has trailing stems to 1 ft. long and thick leaves; summer flowers age from yellow to red. *S. spathulifolium* produces light yellow flowers spring to summer; spoon-shaped blue-green leaves are tinged reddish purple and packed into rosettes on short, trailing stems. *S. spurium* has trailing stems, thick leaves that are dark green or bronze tinted; summer flowers are pink, in dense clusters.

SILENE
HARDINESS VARIES. ☼ ◑ SUN OR PARTIAL SHADE, WATER NEEDS VARY BY SPECIES.

Many species, some cushionlike, some with erect growth habit; most are suitable for rock garden. *S. acaulis* (Cushion pink, Moss campion), hardy to −40°F/−40°C, makes a mosslike mat of small, narrow, bright green leaves; reddish purple, ½-in. flowers are borne singly in spring; needs regular water. *S. schafta* (Moss campion), hardy to −10°F/−23°C, forms tufts of upright, rather wiry stems, to 6–12 in. tall; small, tongue-shaped leaves; flowers are rose purple, one or two to a stalk, late summer into fall; needs moderate water.

VERONICA. Speedwell
0°F/−18°C, EXCEPT AS NOTED. ☼ SUN, WATER NEEDS VARY BY SPECIES.

Handsome plants ranging from 4 in. to 2½ ft. high. *V. incana* (Silver speedwell), hardy to −30°F/−34°C, makes furry, silvery white, mat-forming clumps; deep blue flowers on 10-in. stems in summer. *V. liwanensis,* an evergreen, creeping ground cover to 1 in. tall, has tiny, deep green leaves, bright blue flowers in midspring; needs only enough water to prevent wilting. *V. pectinata* spreads by creeping stems into a prostrate mat; profuse spring or early summer bloom of deep blue flowers with white centers; needs moderate to little water.

ZAUSCHNERIA CALIFORNICA. California fuchsia, Hummingbird flower
0°F/−18°C. ☼ ◕ ◑ SUN, REGULAR TO LITTLE WATER.

Profuse summer-fall bloom of trumpet-shaped, orange to scarlet flowers, to 2 in. long. Stems upright or somewhat arching, 1–2 ft. tall. 'Dublin' ('Glasnevin') is smaller, to 1 ft. tall, and has scarlet flowers. 'Etteri', to 6 in. high, has silvery leaves and scarlet flowers. Also sold as *Epilobium canum canum.*

MAIL-ORDER SOURCES FOR ROCK GARDEN PLANTS

LAPORTE AVENUE NURSERY
Kirk Fieseler
1950 Laporte Avenue
Fort Collins, CO 80521
Catalog $1

MOUNT TAHOMA NURSERY
Rick Lupp
28111 112th Avenue E.
Graham, WA 98338
(253) 847-9827
www.backyardgardener.com/mttahoma
e-mail: RLupp@aol.com
Catalog $2

PORTERHOWSE FARMS
41370 S.E. Thomas Road
Sandy, OR 97055
(503) 668-5834
www.porterhowse.com
e-mail: phfarm@aol.com
Availability and price list is free; Manual of Dwarf & Rare Conifers $6

ROSLYN NURSERY
211 Burrs Lane
Dix Hills, NY 11746
(516) 643-9347;
fax (516) 427-0894
www.roslynnursery.com
e-mail:
roslyn@roslynnursery.com
Catalog $3

SISKIYOU RARE PLANT NURSERY
2825 Cummings Road
Medford, OR 97501
(541) 772-6846;
fax (541) 772-4917
www.wave.net/upg/srpn
e-mail: srpn@wave.net
Catalog $3

TRENNOLL NURSERY
Jim and Dorothy Parker
3 West Page Avenue
P.O. Box 125
Trenton, OH 45067-1614
(513) 988-6121;
fax (513) 988-7079
Catalog $1

WE-DU NURSERIES
Route 5, Box 724
Marion, NC 28752
(828) 738-8300;
fax (828) 738-8131
www.we-du.com
e-mail: wedu@wnclink.com
Catalog $2

THE NORTH AMERICAN ROCK GARDEN SOCIETY

The North American Rock Garden Society has 4,500 members, including new gardeners as well as rock gardening experts. Membership costs $25 a year. Members receive the *Rock Garden Quarterly* and an annual seed list. Other benefits include local meetings and a book lending library. Write to Jacques Mommens, Executive Secretary, P.O. Box 67, Millwood, NY 10546, or find the information at the society's website: www.nargs.org

DWARF CONIFERS

One or two dwarf conifers towering over a carpet of diminutive plants can instantly establish in a rock garden the scale and theme of an alpine landscape. The conifers complete the picture by adding height, mass, and depth to the mats of small plants hugging the ground. If you buy a couple of dwarf conifers, you'll also need less stone, the other main structural element in a rock garden. But limit yourself to just one or two unless your rock garden is large.

ABIES BALSAMEA 'NANA'. Dwarf balsam fir
–40°F/–40°C. ☼ ◐ ● ● SUN OR LIGHT SHADE,
REGULAR TO MODERATE WATER.

Dark green, soft needles, with legendary fragrance. Cones upright, on top of branches. Flattish branches grow 2 in. a year. Does not thrive in hot-summer climates.

CEDRUS DEODARA 'PENDULA' ('PROSTRATA')
0°F/–18°C. ☼ ● SUN, MODERATE WATER.

Gray-green foliage grows flat on ground or will drape over rock or wall; growth rate about 7 in. a year. Branches can be thinned to expose gray-barked trunk, which becomes thick, heavy, and ancient-looking in a very few years. Tolerates hot, humid climates.

CHAMAECYPARIS OBTUSA 'NANA GRACILIS'. Slender Hinoki false cypress
–20°F/–29°C. ☼ ◐ ● SUN OR PARTIAL SHADE,
REGULAR WATER.

Slender, upright, or pleasantly uneven pyramidal growth to 4 ft. with nodding branch tips. Black-green, scale-like leaves in sprays like cupped, upturned hands. Needs good drainage and protection from wind to do well.

JUNIPERUS CHINENSIS PROCUMBENS 'NANA'. Dwarf Japanese garden juniper.
–20°F/–29°C. ☼ ◐ ● ● SUN, TOLERATES LIGHT SHADE,
REGULAR TO MODERATE WATER.

Feathery yet substantial blue-green foliage. Curved branches spread in all directions to make mound 1 ft. high, 4–5 ft. across. Can be staked into upright, picturesque shrub. Also sold as *J. compacta* 'Nana', *J. procumbens* 'Compacta Nana', and *J. procumbens* 'Nana'. Give protection in hot climates.

JUNIPERUS COMMUNIS SAXATILIS
–40°F/–40°C. ☼ ◐ ● ● SUN, TOLERATES LIGHT SHADE,
REGULAR TO MODERATE WATER.

Variable gray, gray-green foliage. Upturned branchlets like tiny candles. Forms prostrate, creeping mat, to 1 ft. high by 6–8 ft. wide. Also sold as *J. c. montana* and *J. c. sibirica.*

Juniperus communis

Pinus mugo mugo

Pinus strobus 'Nana'

JUNIPERUS HORIZONTALIS. Creeping juniper
–20°F/–29°C. ☼ ◐ ● ● SUN, TOLERATES LIGHT SHADE, REGULAR TO MODERATE WATER.

Many named forms, all ground hugging and fast growing—about 8 in. a year. 'Bar Harbor' has blue-gray foliage that turns plum color in winter. 'Douglasii' (Waukegan juniper) has steel blue foliage that turns purplish in fall, and rich green new growth. 'Plumosa' (Andorra juniper) is particularly feathery; foliage is gray-green in summer, plum color in winter. All three grow to 1 ft. tall ('Plumosa', a little taller) and spread to 10 ft.

PICEA ABIES, DWARF FORMS. Norway spruce
–20°F/–29°C. ☼ ◐ ● ● SUN OR LIGHT SHADE,
REGULAR TO MODERATE WATER.

Tolerate wind and some heat and humidity. 'Nidiformis' is low plant with a flat top; at 8 years, it is 2 ft. across, 1 ft. high. 'Sherwoodii' is rugged, picturesque shrub with compact but irregular habit; it was developed from a tree that at age 60 was only 5 ft. tall and 10 ft. across at base.

PICEA GLAUCA 'CONICA'.
Dwarf Alberta spruce, Dwarf white spruce
–40°F/–40°C. ☼ ◐ ● ● SUN OR LIGHT SHADE, REGULAR TO MODERATE WATER.

A dense cone, slowly reaching 7 ft. in 35 years. Short, soft needles are bright grass green when new, gray green when mature. Needs shelter from cold drying wind and strong reflected sunlight. Also sold as *P. albertiana.*

PINUS MUGO MUGO. Mugho pine
30°F/–34°C. ☼ ● ● SUN, REGULAR TO LITTLE WATER.

Shrubby, symmetrical little pine, with dark green needles. Grows slowly to 4 ft. Pick plants with dense, pleasing form.

PINUS STROBUS 'NANA'.
Dwarf white pine
–30°F/–34°C. ☼ ● ● SUN, REGULAR TO LITTLE WATER.

Broad bush twice as wide as tall, with soft, blue-green needles. Grows very slowly to 3–7 ft.

GLOSSARY

Aggregate. Small, round stones, often varicolored, that are seeded into wet concrete to make an attractive surface.

Alpine plants. Plants native to mountain slopes above the tree line; typically require quick drainage and lean soil.

Ashlar. Square-cut stone that can be laid in courses like brick.

Backfill. Soil that has been dug out from one spot and filled into another; it doesn't offer the uniform support of undisturbed earth.

Batter. The inward tilting of the face of a stone wall; it improves the wall's structural stability.

Belgian blocks. Roughly cut stone blocks, similar in size to a large brick; can be laid like cut stone.

Bond stone, or tie stone. A large stone that extends the thickness of a stone wall, tying the faces together.

Cement, portland. A manufactured product, a basic ingredient in both mortar and concrete.

Cobblestones. Roughly cut stone blocks, larger than bricks, once used for street paving; can be laid like cut stone. Or large pebbles, naturally rounded.

Coping. Flat stone used to make a finished top to a wall or a neat edge to a pool.

Course. A single horizontal layer of stones in a stone wall.

Crazy paving. Paving made of irregularly shaped flagstone.

Curing. Keeping mortar or concrete moist for several days while it hardens.

Cut stone. Sawn rectangles and squares of stone that are flat on one or both sides.

Decomposed granite, d.g. Naturally broken stone particles ranging in size from small gravel to sand.

Dry-stone wall. A stone wall built without mortar; it depends upon the weight and friction of one stone on another for stability.

Fieldstone. Stones culled from fields or old walls, irregular in shape and size with aged, uncut faces.

Flagstone. A generic term for flat slabs of paving stone, usually sandstone, limestone, or slate, which split easily; it may have irregular edges or be cut into squares and rectangles.

Footing. A below-ground concrete slab or gravel-bed foundation that supports a stone wall.

Form. A wooden frame built to contain cast concrete while it hardens.

Frost heave. The movement in soil caused by the soil water alternately freezing and thawing.

Gravel. Two kinds: small naturally round stones, like pea gravel, suitable only for a paving surface; and mechanically crushed stone, in various small sizes, such as $5/8$ minus ($5/8$-in. pieces and smaller), suitable for path and dry-stone wall foundations because it packs well, and path surfaces.

Ground fault circuit interrupter, GFI or GFCI, outlet. Outdoor electrical box, with waterproof cover and circuit designed to break, within $1/40$ of a second, if a leak develops in the current.

Liner protection fabric. A nonwoven geotextile that is extremely resistant to tearing.

Mortar. The "glue" used to bond stones together; typically composed of water, lime or fireclay, portland cement, and sand. Mortar can stain stone, so clean up spills quickly.

Muriatic acid solution. Removes mortar smears but may change the color of the stone; don't use on limestone or marble. Prepare with caution, wearing rubber gloves, goggles, and mask; add acid slowly to water—never the reverse.

Quarried rock. Has raw, broken surfaces, suitable mostly for functional paving and walls.

River rock. Stone made smooth by the action of water; ranges in size from gravel to small boulders.

Rubble stone. Any type of uncut stone; it is used in walls but is too irregular to lay in courses.

Runoff. Rainwater or irrigation water moving over the soil or paving surface.

Scree. A pile of flaked or fragmented stone found at the base of cliffs or on mountain ridges, a natural home for many rock garden plants.

Stretcher stone. Long stones that are laid, a few to every course, on the face of a wall.

Tamp. To compact sand, gravel, or soil using the back of a spade, a metal tamper, a water-fillable drum roller, or a rented power vibrator.

Threshold stone. A large or attractive stone at the beginning of a path or at a path intersection.

Veneer stone. Split stone that is used to give a stone face to a concrete block wall.

INDEX

Page numbers in **boldface** refer to photographs.